A Little to the Right

By

James William Huckaby
"Mr. Huck"

James William Huckaby
"Mr. Huck"

DEDICATION

To everything there is a season and
A time to every purpose under Heaven,
A time to weep and a time to laugh,
A time to mourn and a time to dance.
Ecclesiastes 3:1-4

I dedicate this to my Mary. She's my lover, my playmate, and my best friend of all. With you, all my life is a dance, and I can only pray the music continue for all time. Yes, my thanks go to "Pinky", for teaching me to love with the Agape love of Jesus Christ.

"Many people will walk in and out of your life,
But only true friends will leave footprints in your heart"
- Eleanor Roosevelt

TABLE OF CONTENTS

PROLOGUE

Sunsets, like childhood, are viewed with wonder;
not just because they are beautiful,
but because they are fleeting.
The most important story we will ever write in life
is our own;
not with ink, but with our daily choices.
- Richard Paul Evans

And it's winter before you know it...

REFLECTIONS

You know, time has a way of moving quickly and catching you unaware of the passing years. It seems just yesterday that I was young, And yet in a way, it seems like eons ago, and I wonder where all the years went. I know that I lived them all...

And I have glimpses of how it was back then and of all my hopes and dreams... But, here it is.. the winter of my life and it catches me by surprise...
How did I get here so fast? Where did the years go... And where did my youth go? I remember well... seeing older people through the years and thinking that those older people were years away from me and that winter was so far off that I could not fathom it or imagine fully what it would be like.

Each day now, I find that just getting a shower is a real target for the day! And taking a nap is not a treat anymore...it's mandatory! Cause if I don't on my own free will...I just fall asleep where I sit! And so, now I enter into this new season of my life unprepared for all the aches and pains and the loss of strength and ability to go and do things. But, at least I know, that though the winter has come, and I'm not sure how long it will last...This I know, that when it's over...its over....Yes , I have regrets .There are things I wish I hadn't done ,,,,,things I should have done. But indeed, there are many things I'm happy to have done Its all in a lifetime.. .

So, if you're not in your winter yet...let me remind you, that it will be here faster than you think. So, whatever you would like to accomplish in your life please do it quickly! Life goes by quickly So, do what you can today, because you can never be sure whether this is your winter or not! You have no promise that you will see all the seasons of your life...so, live for good today and say all the things that you want your loved ones to remember..."Life is a gift to you. The way you live your life is your gift to those who came after. Make it a fantastic one." LIVE IT WELL!!
~author unknown~

James William Huckaby
"Mr. Huck"

Chapter I

A LOST LOVE

"I have never felt truly at ease around the clean,
shiny, people of this world.
Life has taught me the most trustworthy and
honest are those who are frayed around the edges.
Not always but usually."
- Richard Paul Evans

John & Fanny McCall

"She lives up there on the top of the hill, she's the old lady who has got the religion" they say. You know she's the one that teaches the Belridge Daily Vacation Bible School every summer. She is kind of strange." That is what all the kids used to say, and I was ready to poke

1

someone in the eye at times. When I said something to grandma Finley about it, she would just say, "Buddy that's right, I do got religion. My religion is about LOVE, the kind of love Paul writes about in Corinthians 13:13 (which says and now these three remain: faith, hope, and love. The greatest of these is love). That is my kind of religion Buddy, LOVE." Buddy was her nickname for me.

As I look at the shelf of my bookcase, I see a well worn New Testament that reads on the first page, "1932 - presented to Billie Huckaby for perfect attendance at the Belridge Daily Vacation Bible School.

To get to know my granny you had to know a little bit about her parents, my great-grandparents, John and Fanny McCall. They lived in Fresno in a small house on the south side of the street. Their house was built on the very south end of their lot, with a driveway on the west side from the street to the house with a big vegetable garden on the east side of the driveway that ran from the house to the street.

The school, named Chester Rowell, where I went to the first grade, was only about a block away. Mother would meet me after school and we would walk to their house for something cold to drink before walking on home. If we were lucky, Grandpa would play his fiddle for us. He played a great fiddle, mostly old church tunes. I am thinking that he might have been about the age I am now, ninety years old. He also was about the size and weight I am now. I think I have a little more hair than he did, and he had a few grays around a large bald spot on top.

James William Huckaby
"Mr. Huck"

Irby & Leona

When he died his obituary said that he had been a mining engineer, which did not surprise me because his yard was full of old rocks that looked as if they had just come out of a mine somewhere. One time, I'm not sure I remember why, I spent an entire afternoon with him. He would pick up one of his rocks and examined it carefully, then nodded his head and say, "This is a good one, it's got color". He took his little pickaxe, busted off a good size chunk, and broke it up into smaller pieces until it was like powder. He put the powder into a miners pan and with some water; he washed the water slowly over the powder. He stopped and said, "Look - here's gold". He would carefully pick it out and then wash some more. We did that all afternoon and I had a very small little pile of gold to take home.

My Grandpa had his own way to beat the Fresno heat on very hot days. After dark on hot nights, he would strip down to his nothings and skinny dip in the middle of his vegetable garden with the garden hose and take a nice cool shower. Well that worked very good, and the only one who knew about it was his wife Fanny; until one night we were in the car coming for a visit, and as my Dad turned the car into the driveway, the lights from the car caught a strange nude figure running toward the back of the house. Do you think my Dad ever let Grandpa forget that? I don't think so.

My great-grandparents had a very large family. I think my uncle Bob might have been the oldest; then my grandmother Leona, followed by about four more girls, my uncle Joe, and then another girl Myrtle.

Uncle Bob worked for Sun Maid Raisin Company most of his life. Uncle Joe worked for P.G.& E. in the gas department; and from time to time, I graded some gas pipe for him. From the little bit that I observed as a youth, I would say the entire family was raised as a very solid Christian family. I would bet my last peso that the whole family was Charter Members of The Bethel Temple Pentecostal Church in Fresno (CA). I would believe that my grandmother Leona was raised with the spirit of LOVE in her heart. Any questions about it, then you should see John in his best suit and tie with a bible in hand; and at his side would be Fanny in a beautiful dress with her purse and bible in-hand marching down the street to Bethel Temple, a block away, every Sunday morning. I truly believe most of my grandma's bible knowledge came from the teachings of great-grandma Fanny.

James William Huckaby
"Mr. Huck"

I am not sure how my Dad's parents, George and Leona
Huckaby had met, but I have a guess that I will share
with you. My father was born in the mining town of
Jerome (AZ). Back in 1850, one of the largest gold
mines in the state was in Jerome. I know Dad's father
George was a miner because he had some mining
claims in the hills east of Sanger that Dad had to sign-off
when they built Pine Flat Dam. Now knowing that
Grandpa McCall was a mining engineer, it seems
possible that they all met in Jerome. Over the years,
George and Leona had five children; sons George, John,
Arthur, and William, and daughter Francis. I never knew
grandma to ever call any of her boys by name; she
called all of them Buddy, just like she called me, her only
grandson, Buddy.

George senior, at about age 40, died of pneumonia
leaving Leona alone to raise their five children. Now the
mystery thickens. Where did Irby Finley come from?
Irby was a very religious man and I can only assume that
Irby and Leona met at Bethel Temple, eventually
married, and moved to Belridge. Irby and Leona had a
girl, Lenora, who was about a year older than me. The
boys have all gone leaving Irby, Grandma, Francis, and
Lenora living together at Belridge. Irby's parents lived at
Belridge, and old Grandpa Finley worked for the
company ever since the company started (I think). Irby
had a brother, Bill, who had three children which
Grandma and Grandpa raised after Bill's wife died. One
was a boy named John, about a year older than myself.
One time, I thought he was my bodyguard when he was
about to knock a kids head off for calling me Billy Goat.
It was about this time which I have my first memory of
my Grandma Leona. It was one Saturday afternoon,

and we went to Shafter to a dairy farm to get five gallons of milk, then to a store to buy several loaves of day-old bread. Then we all went home and had fresh milk and bread for dinner for several days. She would repeat this whenever food got a little tight.

I think it was late 1933 or early 1934 that the dust bowl hit the states of Oklahoma, Kansas, and Arkansas; all of the farm workers and their large families were starving and started a rush to California. Some of them ended up in the area of Shafter, Wasco, Buttonwillow, and all the areas around Bakersfield.

Grandma's heart went out to all these large families living in shacks made from cardboard, old pieces of wood, and had to bring in water from miles away. She helped them with food and clothing. She decided that these people needed a church because many of these people loved the Lord just as she did.

The little town of Buttonwillow was only twelve miles away. She checked and found that the town had only one small Baptist Church. She felt the town needed another church so she bought a corner lot in the city. Next, she bartered with some nearby oil companies for an old building. She found one that had been an old bunk-house that she could have if she would move it away, and move it she did. She, along with all the help she could get, opened up the insides to make one large room, and added a stage for a choir, loft, and preaching area. She built a bunch of benches with wooden backs and soon opened up the Buttonwillow Pentecostal Church.

I would like to say that crowds flooded in but it wasn't

true, the church grew slowly, but it did grow.
Buttonwillow was the end of the line for the railroad, and
many of the young male riders would come into the
church just to get warm. But before they left they had
heard Grandma preach, and they were encouraged to
give their lives to Christ. These were the people
Grandma loved with God's love. Auntie Francis played a
kind of mean piano, one of the "Okie" families came and
the father played an old guitar that his pick had worn a
hole in the side. Little Jimmy (one of the people from
town) played a great Banjo. There were a couple of
families who came over from Taft for Sunday night
services and one of the men had a beautiful big guitar
that added a bit of class. It wasn't long before Grandma
had them dancing in the spirit and marching around the
room, like a bunch of army recruits singing "When the
Saints Go Marching In".

The other family from Taft was "Brother Thickle" and his
wife. He was known far and wide for his testimony of
how Christ had saved him. When the spirit came over
him he got excited and shared and shared and shared.
He was a tall man with a large mouth full of teeth, and
sometimes his spit flew to the third row. At the same
time, his little wife was crouching down in her seat
wondering when he was going to stop. Brother Darryl
and his younger brother Tilton started coming to the
Pentecostal Church. Darryl was the Buttonwillow
Postmaster, and a member in good standing of the
Buttonwillow Baptist Church. They became regular
attendees.

One Sunday morning two young men come in out of the
cold, they had just come into town in a box-car the night
before. Grandma greeted them and later preached to

them, and after the service she invited them to Belridge for dinner. On the ride home, a jack rabbit ran in front of the car and got hit, landing its body on the front bumper. When we got home one of the men spotted the rabbit, pulled out his knife, skinned and dressed it out and said, "This will make me a nice stew tonight." After dinner and a nice nap, we all headed back for Sunday night services.

The old pants story has been told to death, but it needs a space here. One weekend, Dad, Mom, my sister Betty, and I were at grandma's house. We got up to get ready for church. Dad had two pair of dress pants: a pair of blue and a pair of gray. He could find the blue but not the gray. He asked grandma if she knew of the loss. Grandma replied, "Buddy, brother White had stopped coming to church because he had no dress pants, so I gave him your gray ones. You only need one pair of dress pants anyway." Brother White was a young black man who came to town on the rails two weeks prior. To Grandma, if there was a need there was always a way!

The year is 1935, Irby and grandmother were visiting her family in Fresno. Leona is suddenly having discomfort with an infected tooth and ends up in a hospital in Fresno. The tooth continues to get worse, and would eventually take her life. Where were the antibiotics that we have today that would've probably saved her life? What a loss to her family. What a loss to the souls that might have been saved through her ministry, and most importantly, what a total loss it was for me. I loved her dearly. I always wanted to please her in everything I did. I have often wondered where I would be today if she had lived a few more years. Some of the influences she had on my life I live with still today.

James William Huckaby
"Mr. Huck"

*"I WILL DANCE WITH MARY
TO THOSE WONDERFUL TUNES
OF THE 40's & 50's; AND IF I AT THE SAME TIME,
WISH TO WEEP OVER A LOST LOVE…, I WILL"*
- Author unknown

Chapter Two

A NEW HOME - A NEW LIFE

*"From our first infant babblings to our last word we
make are but one statement, and that is our life.
One cannot make laws to rule the heart."*
Richard Paul Evans

It's a nice warm sunny afternoon in Fresno, the year is
probably 1928 and two seven years boys are coming out
of the front door of the Chester Rowell School. They
cross the street and head south. Normally, my mother
and baby sister would meet me, and we would go to
great-grandmother's for a cold drink. But today my sister
was sick, so I and my little friend Bobby would just walk
the two blocks home.

Being in first grade, we were quite happy that we had the
freedom to walk home by ourselves. We walked along
basically just having fun kicking up dust and throwing
rocks. We noticed the old water tank house off to the
right at a little distance. We had seen it there and
passed by it time and again, but today we were in no
hurry so we thought it would be a great time to go over
and investigate a little.

The building is old and rotted; it needs paint and the
shingles are falling off the roof. It has a door on the
south side and windows on the east and west sides.
The tank loft has windows on the east and west also.
We decided that a building that old doesn't need good
windows like that, so we chuck a few rocks at the
window on the west side which can't be seen from the

road. As luck would have it, we were successful and crash goes the window. Then we look up at the big challenge - the upstairs window. We need something bigger to throw, so one boy finds a large old rusty iron file (I really don't remember which of us), just the thing we needed. After a few tosses they hit the mark, the window crashes, but when the iron file hit the old empty water tank, it let out a big bang like a clap of thunder that scares these two bravados. Their guardian angel says, "I think I would run", and run WE did, as fast as four little legs could go.

Now I remember the crime very well but; for the life of me, 90 years later, I cannot remember what our punishment was. I do know my father paid for two new windows for the old tank house. I remember also that any time I walked to school alone, I took the opposite side of the street. Those two windows on the east side of the tank house would glare at me and say, "you wouldn't dare", and I would always walk just a little faster to get past.

The Great Depression hit the world in 1929, and is commonly used as an example of how far the world's economy can decline. It originated in the United States, starting with the decline in stock prices beginning around September 4, 1929, and became worldwide news with the stock market crash on October 29, of the same year. From there it quickly spread and had devastating effects on almost every country in the world. Unemployment in the United States rose to 25%, while some countries hit as high as 33%. Construction was virtually halted, farming and rural areas suffered as crop prices fell by approximately 60%, and jobs suffered the most.

James William Huckaby
"Mr. Huck"

Prior to 1929, my father had dependable work driving for a freight company that hauled the big electrical generators into the new power houses of San Joaquin Power and Light Company in the Sierra Mountains. The first memories I have of difficulties caused by the depression were in the later part of 1931. My father had lost his job, we had been put out of our rented house, and Mom, Dad, Betty, and I were in Dad's one seat model 'T' Ford headed for grandmothers at Belridge.

When we arrived we found that grandma's house walls were bulging at the seams. Grandma and Irby, with their two girls Francis and Lenora, and Dad's two brothers Art and Bill were all there. However Bill thought he had a job coming soon. At the end of the week it was decided that I would stay there in Belridge, and Dad would take Mom and Betty back to Sanger to Grandma Wilson's to stay on the farm. Irby kept his job with Belridge Oil Company all through the depression years; so thanks to him we always had a little food on the table. Sometimes it was just bread and milk, but we all remained healthy. I remember the long evenings with grandma lying in bed with me on one side and Lenora on the other reading Bible Stories night after night.

I have no idea how my father survived the streets of Fresno, but survive he did and a few months later he found work. Unexpectedly there appeared at Belridge an old model 'T' Ford (this Ford might have been where Dad slept in Fresno). Mom, Dad, and Betty were ready to take me to our new home. Not long ago I noticed in looking at my Bible School New Testament written in red ink, "If found, return to 731 Roosevelt." This was the last house on the street, and my new home. It was here where my Uncle Charles and Dad decided to make their own beer. It was during prohibition when alcoholic beverages were illegal. However, after they made their beer, they hid it under the house. Irby and Grandma came for a surprise overnight visit, and during the night several bottles of the fermented beer under the house exploded; it sounded like a war under grandma's bedroom and she thought she had been shot. How Dad explained that I never heard!

It was at this house that Mother and Dad worked up the back yard. Mother had a beautiful flower garden; some of her flowers were head high. Along the side of the house, between the house and the driveway, she planted what she called hen and chicks (a draught tolerant flower) the full length of the house. During this time Dad had showed me how to drive the Model T Ford up and down the driveway for him. You guessed it; I got to close to the house and killed all of Mom's hens and chickens. Even in those days mother could discipline with just that special look she had.

I started the third grade at John Muir School while we lived there. However, I didn't get very far because once again we were out of a house because Dad had lost his job and we were out of rent money. While we were in Fresno, Dad traded the Model 'T' Ford for a one seat Modal 'A' Ford, and the four of us were headed for Belridge for another stay. This time Mother, Betty, and I all would stay and Dad was back to Fresno one more time to look for work.

By this time Aunt Francis had married a man from Mississippi and moved out. Uncle Art married a girl from Taft and was long gone. There was just Irby, Grandma, and Lenora there, so the three of us fit in very nicely. It was a good thing as it ended up that this stay was quite lengthy. Grandma's dream of a church in Buttonwillow was completed and holding three services a week. The three of us became regular attendees in the church and it was at this time that Mother and I gave our lives to Christ.

At the risk of losing a few of you who have a problem with baptism and tongues and such, I feel that I must share the following story of my life. My limited theology doesn't totally explain it all, but I can give you some scriptures that might help. I was eleven years old at the time and when I told my grandmother I had given my life to Christ, she was very happy. Then she said, "Now you must pray for the baptism of the Holy Spirit." I began to pray for the Holy Spirit and on about the third night it happened. I opened my eyes and I was lying on the floor with my head in my grandmother's lap. She was sitting on the floor with me. She said, "Buddy, you just received the Holy Spirit." My mother said I was lying on the floor waving my arms talking in tongues like I was preaching to some one. My little seven year old sister thought I had gone crazy.

Now please let me quote some scriptures that come from my bible.

First, chapter 14 of 1st Corinthians talks about gifts of prophecy and tongues and verse 1 says to, "...eagerly desire spiritual gifts". Tongues is one of the spiritual gifts mentioned there. Acts chapter 2 describes the Holy Spirit coming at Pentecost, and verse 4 says, "All of them were filled with the Holy Spirit and began to speak in other tongues as the Spirit enabled them". Acts chapter 19 verse 5 says, "They were baptized into the name of the Lord Jesus the Holy Spirit came on them and they spoke in tongues".

If this little story has disagreed with some ones theology I am so sorry, but at the age of 11, this is what happened to me, and I believe, "God meets us right where we are." My grandmother had no seminary training, she had none of the great theologians that we have today to train and teach her scriptures. She had only two of God's greatest gifts to help and direct her: the Holy Spirit and the Bible. I believe because of the way she interpreted and preached the scriptures, there are many people in heaven today. In my adult life, I have relied on the Holy Spirit to help me make many of the important decisions I have made. So please read on; the stories and memories may get better.

It was probably the summer of 1934 when my father got work driving for a trucking firm, and moved us back to a rented house on Effie Street in Fresno. This change lasted only three months: my father's job was gone and we were back at grandma's house in Belridge again. Thank God for grandma and Irby. My father was back on the streets in Fresno looking for work again.

Sometime in late 1934 or early 1935 when The Buttonwillow Pentecostal Four Square Church had a Brush Arbor Festival after a Sunday morning service to be held at the Jones farm east of town. There was to be a baptismal service in the Jones reservoir in the mid-afternoon. Everyone was welcome to bring friends and family, so a large crowd with many new people we had never seen before came for food and fun. Grandma always wore a white uniform to church services and when the time was right she got up with her bible, read some scriptures, and then walked over to the reservoir and waded into the waist high water. She baptized all the people who wished to be baptized, one of which was the Postmaster of Buttonwillow who had belonged to the Baptist Church, and had now become a regular attendant at our church.

After the last adults were baptized, grandma looked at me and motioned it was my turn. Just twelve years old, I waded out to meet her. She said the words that needed to be said, then bent me over backwards and pulled me back up and gave me a hug and a kiss. None of the others got the hug and kiss because I was her only grandson; in fact, my sister and I were grandma's only grandchildren. From now on this Four Square Church would be my church - my first church. The following Sunday we had a couple of missionaries from South America sharing about their work. I knew then that when I grew up I was going to be a missionary in South America.

After another lengthy stay at grandma's house, my father again found work and moved us back to Fresno. This would be our last house in Fresno, and it was also on Roosevelt Avenue only much further north. Once again I went to the John Muir School, but this time it was to the fifth grade. Two doors down lived a little girl that was in the fifth grade also. Her name was Permelia, she played the accordion and danced – she was my first love. One weekend, Mother and Dad were gone and my Grandma Wilson was staying with us. Permelia ask if I could go to a movie with her, I asked Grandma and she thought it was alright, so off we went. When Mother got back and I told her what had happened she said, "Buddy don't ever do that again, going to a movie is a big sin." Funny, I thought that holding hands in that movie theater with Permelia was heaven to me; I could see no sin there.

Like thousands and thousands of other people from 1931 until 1935, our lifestyle was one of much unrest. It was a constant battle of beating the streets trying to find work, and if you did find a job, how long would it last? We lived in four furnished rental houses during that period; fortunately, we had no furniture to move. It was just 'grab your clothes and go' when your rent money ran out. Thank God that Irby and Grandma were there when my father needed a place for us.

My father never complained about how he lived and survived all those times he was alone in Fresno trying to find a little work. He made sure we were taken care of first, and then found some way to take care of himself. My Dad was the kind of person who said, "bite the bullet, get out there find work, and get my family back." I have no idea how he survived those long days and nights in Fresno alone.

Grandma's unexpected death put everyone in total confusion. She had been a complete rock that everyone turned to in times of trouble. Probably the hardest hit was Irby, finding himself a single parent with a twelve year old daughter to raise. It was time to repay him for his generous help during those depression years. So once again, we are on the move to help pick up the shattered pieces. Irby and Lenora end up at grandma's house, and our family ends up there as well. Lenora will go to a Christian School in Modesto and will be home during the summer months, and mother will cook for all of us. Dad has at last found a permanent job working for Belridge Oil Company. Now we had a new life, a home of our own, a school that we could attend, and we were all ready to try it without grandma.

A year or so later, Irby found a new wife, and he and Lenora moved to Wasco. However, the furniture at Belridge belonged to Irby and he needed some of it to furnish his new home. I have no idea what he took, but our father was off to McMahon's furniture store in Bakersfield and signed his life away. I do not remember all that we got, but one thing I do remember was a beautiful standing RCA RADIO. We listened to Jack Armstrong the All American Boy, Orphan Annie, Tom Mix, and The Lone Ranger.

Dad had a big heart for his children while Mom questioned if we really needed it. We still drove around in our one seat Model A Ford. Dad driving, Mom in the middle with Betty on her lap, and me squeezed in on the side. Life was good. On our first Christmas in Belridge I got my first bicycle and Betty got lots of nice girl gifts. We were in hog heaven. We never did go back to grandma's church in Buttonwillow. I only had the memory of receiving the Holy Spirit there for years and years. None of grandma's boys were very keen on church, not even Dad; he would only go when grandma insisted. The second oldest John moved his family to Texas when I was too young to remember. I heard in later years he died an alcoholic. I know for a fact that the other three boys died knowing the Lord. Uncle Art had three wives during a twenty-five year span; and a daughter with his second wife. Uncle Bill also had three wives but over about a thirty year span, and he had two boys with his first wife.

It was about this time we noticed that Mom was filling out

in her tummy quite a bit. Sure enough she had a little BUN in her oven. After her delivery in the hospital, Mom stayed in a home in Bakersfield for several days with our new baby sister Lois. As the summer got hotter, Lois could not stand the heat so the doctor told Dad he had to get her out of the heat immediately. The next day Dad had us on our way to Pismo Beach, about two hours away, where we stayed for three months. Betty and I had a blast there. Dad put us up in a nice motel and the manager was especially nice to us.

One day he knocked at the door and handed me two empty beer bottles. He told me that if I checked the back doors each morning after the people left, I could pick up the beer bottles and take them down to the store and get five cents a bottle. Just below the motel was an old beach comber's shack. The old man rented surf boards, clamming forks and a few trinkets to sell. He was very kind to me when I came around.

I borrowed a pair of skates from a friend when we left Belridge, and before we returned home I had just about wore them out. I skated all over Pismo that year. We had no sidewalks to skate on at Belridge; the only place was the tennis court and that was not good if some people were trying to play tennis. In years to come a group of us made regular trips to Bakersfield to the Roller Derby. It was so much fun watching those people do Roller Skate Dancing; made me wish I could do it. One day I was swimming in the ocean and I got out a little too far out and as I stood up to walk in to shore, the undertow was so strong it started to pull me under. Fortunately there was a man close by that grabbed my arm and got me back up to the beach. I never told Mom about it or she would have put a stop to my swimming alone.

At the end of the summer, I had almost made enough money selling beer bottles to buy my friend some new skates, and we all got back home and settled in for the winter. On the way home Dad discovered the apples for sale in Atascadero. You bought them by the tree and had to pick everything on the tree yourself. We went home and the next weekend Dad borrowed a trailer and went over and bought two trees. You should have seen all five of us in the front seat of the old Model 'A' Ford pulling a huge trailer load of apples. We brought them home and wrapped each one in paper and we ate apples all winter. I could eat two or three at one setting. We did that year after year for several years. When grandma was alive, there was a man who brought huge truck load of apples from Watsonville every fall; and grandma would feed him and let him stay over night for two boxes of apples. She got two different kinds of apples, one for pies and one for eating.

Somewhere between the 5th and the 8th grades, my teacher Miss Emmy Lou was determined to teach the world's worst speller (me) how to spell. I got out of school at 3:30pm and my father got off work every day at 4:30pm. The hour between, I spent writing my spelling words over and over. Usually on Friday, if I stepped out of the classroom, I would see the old Model 'A' tearing across the country; it meant that Betty and I would find a note on the table saying, "Betty set the table and Bill peel the potatoes." Mom, Dad, and Baby Lois were going to McKittrick to Mrs. Ramsey's grocery store, and we would have a real good meal that night.

At this time in my father's life, I never knew him to pay

anything but cash for everything. I don't know how he made his meager money stretch as far as it did. However, on the first of the month Dad would get his pay check and he would pay in-full the bill he owed for food during the previous month. Then he will gather enough food to last a week and charged it. So for about thirty minutes, he was out of debt until he walked out of the store, owing Mrs. Ramsey, the week's groceries he just picked up. Now you tell me who was the winner there? Anyway, it worked for Dad and Mrs. Ramsey; she always got her money from Dad's next check.

Now with a few bucks still in his pocket, it's down the street to Big Joe's Butcher Shop. Big Joe sees him coming so he goes into his cooler and pulls out a half of a cow. "The usual," Dad says. Joe knows what that means, a fresh one and a half inch cut of round steak. Of course Dad has to visit with Joe while Mom and Lois set in the hot Model 'A' trying to stay cool. "BILL, YOU NOTICE THE CUT?" It's an old Huckaby tradition started in 1935 that was kept by my Dad; which I too have kept it through my lifetime (my son Bill on the other hand discovered that there were other cuts besides round steak that he thought were much better, and broke the tradition). It took Mom just a short time to turn out fried steak and gravy, mashed potatoes, fresh corn, and a big piece of apple pie.

It was up to Betty and I to clean-up the kitchen after dinner. I would wash and Betty would dry and after we got through, I had to sweep the kitchen. Mother and Dad would sit on the sofa while Betty and I fussed, and they listened to our new radio and watched me sweep the floor. One night I had finished and Dad said, "You missed a spot I can see it from here. Sweep it again".

Once more I swept it and Dad said he could, "still see it, sweep it again". This went on and on and I finally discovered that a towel had dropped on the floor behind the table. I had swept around it time and again and when I picked it up and swept, Dad said, "that looks nice now".

One Saturday morning, Dad went out and got into the old Model 'A' by himself and drove off, and was gone until late afternoon. Then here he came driving a beautiful new 1936 Ford. It was a four door sedan a nice soft gray color. It had the spare tire mounted on the back in a nice cover. He said it was our reward for all the time the five of us had ridden in the old Model 'A'.

Dad and his new truck

Dad proved himself to be a good employee for the company, so they bought him a brand new truck, much larger and bigger than the old one.

He was the only one that was allowed to drive it, and at the same time gave him an assistant to help him with his loads. If it sounded like the generators he moved to the mountains in 1929 were big, you should have seen the big gas engines, the huge big tanks, and the long load of drill pipe he moved in and out of the big pumping plants at Belridge! There was nothing to big for him to tackle. It was about this time that the house next to us became available. It was a much larger three bedroom house that faced the Main Street, and Dad and Mom jump at the opportunity. The houses were rented to the employees for a very small amount of money; I think it was less than 20 dollars a month. The company carpenter went in and did some repair work and painted it up like new. Lights, gas, and water were included in the rent. Grandma's house was much smaller, kind of on a little hill, and not even near a street. When cars would drive by on the dirt road it created a lot of dust that mother was glad to get away from in the new house. So move we did, and for me all of grandma's memories left also.

I was in the fifth grade when we left Fresno for good and because of how unsettled we were, my new teacher at Belridge said I should do the fifth grade again. So, that was where I started when we moved. Betty was in the second grade. Miss Barns taught first through fourth. Miss Emmy Lou taught fifth through eighth grades. They were both very good teachers and were there for all our time in grade school.

School had its share of excitement at times, one happened when one of the older boys made a nasty remark about my friend John's Grandma Finley. We

were all standing in a line when "BAM", John laid a hard
right to the nose of a kid and blood shot every where.
The teacher said, "John, I'll deal with you later. You stay
after school." She got the blood stopped and continued
with class. After school, she told John to go out and get
three limbs off a small tree, and when John came back
in, she preceded to give John a whipping. When old
Grandma Finley got wind of what happened, she came
out like a young Fighting Cock and told the teacher to
never lay a hand on one of her grandchildren in the
future; if her children needed correction she would take
care of it herself.

Well, I graduated from the eighth grade with the rest of
my class (another boy and a girl for a total of three) and
we moved on to high school. There was twelve years
difference between Lois and me, and when Lois was
born, Betty and I felt that God had finally smiled on us.
Lois was a beautiful baby and a beautiful child with her
big blue eyes and curly blond hair. She was even a
beautiful teenager, and she is still beautiful today. Lois
was what Betty and I always wished we were; beautiful
and handsome.

In 1941 Dad got another new car, a four door Chevrolet,
maybe for me to impress my dates; I don't think so.
However, he did let me use it when I took Mary to the
Mid-Winter Ball that night. Mary was that cute little
redhead that got on our school bus; which you will read
about later. I don't think she was impressed because all
we saw was the stars in each others eyes.

Betty and I had a short period of time when we had a
special thing going. Belridge built what they called a
Club House. It had a big auditorium with a game room

for cards, and quite frequently we would have dances. Betty and I started dancing together a lot. I would go to a movie that had a lot of dancing and come home with a lot of fancy dance moves. We would learn something new for every dance they had. We had a blast showing off for the old timers. I think that I am safe to say 1935 brought a complete change in our life style. Our old life style was one of unrest, fear, and wonder if the depression would ever end.

So to answer your question, I like being old.
It has set me free. I like the person I have become.
I am not going to live forever, but while I am still here,
I will not waste time lamenting what could have been,
or worry about what will be;
and I shall eat dessert every single day
(if I feel like it).

- Author Unknown

Chapter Three

BELRIDGE

"My mother used to tell me that angels were disguised as people. Tonight I am a believer; stories like babies don't wait for decent hours to be born."
- Richard Paul Evans

South Belridge Oil field is a large oil field in northwestern Kern County. Discovered in 1911, and having a cumulative production of close to 2 billion barrels of oil at the end of 2006, it is the fourth largest oil field in California, and is the sixth most productive field in the United States. Its estimated remaining reserves, as of 2006, were around 520 million barrels, the second-largest in the state, and it has 6,017 active wells. The oil field is located forty miles west of Bakersfield, is about ten miles long by two miles wide, and encompasses 9,420 productive acres. Most native vegetation is gone from the oil field, with the most operational areas being almost completely barren except for pumping units, drilling pads, storage tanks, steam generators, and associated equipment. In spite of this seeming sterility, species such as the endangered San Joaquin Kit Fox continue to use areas of the oil field development as habitat.

A total of six oil pools have been found in South Belridge: The Tulare and Diatomite were discovered in 1911 and are the largest and nearest the surface with average depths of 400 and 1,000 feet respectively. The Antelope Shale at 4,000 feet and the McDonald at 6,700 feet are the deepest working pools. The Devilwater-

Gould was found in 1980 at a depth of 8,200 feet only produced one well for nine months, and then was abandoned. Finally there is the Etchegoin pool. Belridge Oil Company discovered the field and retained control of operations until 1979 when Shell Oil purchased the company along with most of the production rights on the South Belridge Field for $3.65 billion. The Belridge unit claimed a daily production of 140,000 barrels of oil and was the second-largest producer of oil in California by the end of 2006.

North Belridge Oil Field is a large oil field located just eight miles northwest of the larger South Belridge Oil Field, in a region of highly productive and mature fields. Discovered in 1912, it is five miles long and one mile across; it has a cumulative production of almost 137 million barrels of oil as of the end of 2006. It is also estimated to hold 27 million barrels in reserve, making it the 40th largest oil field in the State. Over 2,800 wells had been drilled on the field since its discovery in 1912. It was also acquired by Shell Oil in 1979, but operations were later turned over to Aera Energy, a joint venture of Shell and Mobile Oil Company in 1997. The Belridge Oil Company wasn't the only company to have holdings in the North Field as Associated Oil, Standard Oil, Mobile Oil, and many others were drilling in the same area. Each company built a few homes for the families working in the fields, whereas Belridge Oil provided 15 to 20 homes at the north-end as we used to call it.

South Belridge was the headquarters for Belridge Oil Company and their offices were located there, along with the main warehouse, main garage, carpenters shops, and electrical shops. There was a nice wash rack for employees to wash and clean their cars. There were four big bunk houses each holding ten men with nice bathrooms, and garages for their cars. Across the way was a big cook house for those men serving three meals everyday. They provided approximately forty homes for families, and also built a big clubhouse for dances, plays, school activities, and pot-lucks. There was a beautiful adobe building with an adobe wall around it that housed the corporate bosses when they came in from Los Angles, and a cottage for their drivers. We had a two-room school house and two teachers; and they had a house to live in with a garage. A half mile west of camp on a hill was a swimming pool which opened every afternoon in the summer from 1:00 to 9:00pm with a company life guard. All of the oil companies had softball teams, so we had a nice softball diamond, and a nice tennis court in the middle of camp. We had big old wooden oil derricks all around the camp, jack plants and jack lines pumping the wells, big old shipping plants with big old gas engines popping away. That was Belridge in 1935.

The spring brought miles and miles of beautiful wild flowers. Later, when I got my first bicycle, I would ride through them for hours. The spring also brought the sheep herders with their sheep to graze along the foothills. The herders slept in tents and cooked on open fires. Each one had a burro or donkey that packed his tent and supplies to the next grazing location. One year a herder moved his sheep to a different location in the state, and he left behind his burro Jenny to fend for herself. Little old Jenny would roam into camp from time to time and the kids had a real treat for several days, feeding her and trying to ride her. She was gentle and good with everyone. She would come back two or three times during the winter, but the herder found her when he returned the next year. That was the Belridge that we loved and grew up with.

Over the years I have tried to think how my father felt about Belridge in 1935. Sagebrush, rattlesnakes, dust storms, oil derricks everywhere, big old gas engines puff, puff, puffing away; was this worth trading for the city life in Fresno with it's sidewalks, street cars, and green lawns? One would wonder, could it be possible, after our father had spent years walking those sidewalks looking for work during the depression years, that he would be happy in Belridge? Dad knew Belridge though, because that was where grandma lived, and it was where he left Mother, Betty, and I when he could not make enough money to get a house for us. We did this off and on through those years; grandma was always there for us when we needed her. I know that each time Dad was with us at Belridge he would try to get work from the company only to be denied. Betty and I, from our previous stays at grandma's, already knew most of the kids in the camp, so we just blended in with the group. Do I think our father was concerned about the move for his kids? I don't think so. I think he felt it was a God sent relief, after what we had been through in the past.

Our father is long gone, we lost him in 1982, from a heart attack. So Dad, if there is any doubt in your mind that you made the right decision in 1935, the following two e-mails are just for you.

THINKING
(Written by my sister Betty Huckaby Keeter)

"What can I say about, "Growing up at Belridge"?

James William Huckaby
"Mr. Huck"

Where else could any kid live that could be more wonderful? Everyday was filled with fun.

I remember when we first moved there, I could see that it was going to be a whole lot different than living in Fresno. Gee, no stores or busy streets, only some houses, oil wells, and desert all around us. But it wasn't long that I soon learned that it was going to be a great place to grow up. When I was quite young, I remember how the kids would gather under a street light, and we would play hide-and-seek, or kick-the-can, and all ages played, yelling and screaming until bedtime. There weren't a lot of families that lived there, but there were enough that everyone had good friends, and enjoyed every day. There were no fears, nobody locked a door. There was no place to buy anything or go to a movie, but everyday was filled with good times. We had our school which was across the road from our house, and was where I first met up with Emmy Lou, the head school teacher, and believe me, she could shoot fire out of her eyes, and we were all scared to death of her. BUT, she was there to teach us and make sure that we learned, and we did learn, or stayed after school until we did.

Belridge provided us with a wonderful huge swimming pool, and hired a man who was the lifeguard on-duty every day. Every kid who grew up there could swim very well. Also we had a great tennis court at the school, and we learned to play tennis very well. In fact, my brother Bill was so good that he lettered in tennis at Taft High School. Things were pretty casual at Belridge. None of us wore shoes much, unless we were going to school. I was the rough and tumble kid in our family, always had scabs on both knees. Mother kept wondering and asking me when I "was going to act like a young lady?"

Living across the street from the school was nice as we could come home every day for lunch; but also, it was convenient for our little Bulldog "BOOTS" who'd dash over and grab the kids' ball and run home with it. Then mother would have to answer the knock on the door, and one of the ball players would say, "Mrs. Huckaby, Boots ran away with our ball again.", and mother would have to go in the yard and retrieve it. When I was about nine years old, Mother gave us the most wonderful present Bill and I could ever have received, our beautiful little sister. What a joy she was and every evening Mother would put her in the buggy and the whole family would go for a walk up the road, past old Plant #1, and on out into the rest of the area toward General Petroleum, another oil lease and more friends. We grew up listening to old Plant #1 that was close to our house. It went uga, uga, chugga chugga, wheeze, wheeze, and this went on day and night, but we got used to the noise and never heard it. We kids would hike up to it because we liked to stand next to the cooling tower where there would always be a cool watery mist, and it felt so good in the summer time. We never missed not living in town, and when Dad and Mother would go after groceries, we would usually stay home. Emmy Lou was good at adding entertainment for Belridge people. She tried to make actors out of all us kids, and she put stage plays on every holiday or any special occasion. She also tried her best to make singers out of all of us, so we could perform for the crowd, but she didn't have much to work with in the Huckaby clan. To this day, when I try to sing the dog leaves the room."

Remembering Belridge
(Written by my sister Lois Huckaby Hargrove)
"Well, this has proven to be a lot harder for me. In

looking back I do so love my childhood at Belridge, at the time I just didn't give it a lot of thought. I do remember the Friday night movies at the clubhouse, oh how I loved them. Every summer at noon I was walking barefooted to the swimming pool, staying until supper time and then home. Nine times out of ten my friend Margaret would call and say lets go swimming; so back I would go, boy was I a lucky girl to have a swimming pool for my use. Of course, I got my legs switched with a stick a few times; I could always just roam around the desert and not have one darn thing to worry about. Mama would tell me, "Lois, stay out of the sumps", when I got home I would have tar all over me. And the times that Daddy taught me to chew tar, did I love that? I sure did. And of course how many kids had wooden derricks in their front yard that we would climb every chance we got. Do you remember Tony Jesselneck? Daddy always said the only reason Belridge hired him was to lick the tops of the catch-up bottles. I don't think there was one square inch I didn't walk in Belridge, and even though I got into things, I never really got into trouble; I just rambled all over. I didn't even know what a bum was until I was grown. It was absolutely the safest place to raise kids I can think of; and the school, what fun it was to play tennis, and skate on the tennis court, and do you remember the adobe building where all the big shots stayed and it had the best pomegranate tree ever. And every boyfriend I ever had that was where we would go to get some privacy; that is until Mama would blow that damn whistle, which wasn't a very long time to be with a boy. But, to be truthful, there weren't too many boys who wanted to drive all that way to Belridge. In looking back, I think the only reason I had a boyfriend at all was so they could steal "drip" off the wells for their cars.

I do believe that I had the most wonderful childhood ever. Even with the dreaded tumbleweeds, the size of cars, and the dreaded dust storms (boy those were bad), but we just lived with them and didn't give them a lot of thought. I really don't know anything more, it was all just good times for me. I'm sure at the time I didn't see it that way, being the obnoxious child I was, but now that I am an old lady, I can only say it was a wonderful place to live. I always loved to be outside and walking the desert. I told my husband Bob, the whole time when I was walking that desert I never saw a rattlesnake; I did see lots of tarantulas though and I can remember how I loved to see the tumbleweeds rolling across the desert. I do remember how sad it was to go back after we were married and had our kids, and the house was going to be torn down; it about broke my heart, Mama and I walked thru the house and I think both of us had tears in our eyes. Progress sucks, you want to be able to go and visit your childhood and it was gone."

I sent my sweet sisters an e-mail asking them to share some of their memories of growing up in Belridge. Because their responses were so great and I felt it was right from their hearts, I decided to print them just the way I received them. Thank you both so much.

Well Dad, if you are listening, I think it's obvious that your children agree that the decision you made in 1935 was the best for us. The three of us totally loved our childhood at Belridge. However, ten years later, Mary and I would make a decision about Belridge. Was it where we wanted to raise our children? Three different occasions the head man of Belridge offered me work, but we felt that God had called us to go to Fresno, and to say no to Belridge, which we did.

Some years later, Belridge discovered the two new and deeper oil formations: the Antelope Shale and the McDonald; the Belridge camp was sitting on millions of barrels of oil, and we would have to be moved. They picked a spot about two miles west of the old camp and started building houses.

One day I went from Fresno to Bakersfield to take care of a little chore that took about half a day. After lunch, I decided to drive west to Belridge on my way home. When I got there I wished that I had gone straight home. The camp was a huge mess, the swimming pool on the hill was flat now, about half of the houses were all gone, and it looked like the rest were soon to go. The school house had been leveled, and the tennis court along with it. There was no longer a cook-house or bunk-houses. A bull-dozer was working on the adobe fence and I guessed the building would be next. Old Plant #1 was gone, as well as the old Jack plant, and almost all of the old wooden derricks had been knocked down. The pump jacks were going up and down in every direction you looked, and yes there was one going up and down on the hill where grandma's house used to be.

SICKNENING.

Where was the old Belridge that we had loved so much? The new oil company had shown no sympathy to those who had lived there for so many years. With a very heavy broken heart, I turned my car around and headed back for Fresno and never looked back. I was so glad that my sisters had not seen what had happened to their beloved Belridge. Is there anything sacred anymore?

DAD, WE WERE BOTH RIGHT

I know I am sometimes forgetful. But there again, some of life is just as well forgotten. I eventually remember the important things and I can still dance.

> *"It has been a mistake living my life in the past.*
> *One cannot ride a horse backwards*
> *and still hold its reins."*
> *- Richard Paul Evans*

Chapter   Four

GOALS AND DREAMS

I've come to know that our families are but canvas on which we paint our greatest hopes - imperfect and sloppy, for we are all amateurs at life, but if we do not focus too much on our mistakes, a miraculous picture emerges and we learn that it's not the beauty of the image that warrants our gratitude –
it's the chance to paint.
- Richard Paul Evans

It's the middle of June 1941, and I'm on the high school bus riding home. My high school, Taft High, is 40 miles southwest of Bakersfield. From Taft we traveled about 18 miles north where we stopped in the small oilfield town of McKittrick to drop off about half of the students. Another 12 miles is South Belridge, and this is where I will get off. The bus will travel another 10 miles to North Belridge to finish the trip of 40 miles. For me it is 30 miles twice a day, five days a week for four years. That totals about 46,800 miles to get four years of knowledge.

Could this really be my last trip?

I had gone to my graduation ceremonies last night, I'm 19 years old and I have to make some decisions. I have no money for college, I had worked for Mid-state Petroleum last summer, and they had allowed me to work week-ends during the winter, but they paid only a pittance, and for sure my parents can t send me. I know that Belridge would give me a job if I was ready to go to work.

WHAT DO I DO? WHERE DO I GO? GOD HELP ME.

I was pleased with the way my tennis game had improved over the last four years of High School. With the coaching I had received I had made the team all four years. However, I was no longer happy playing with the kids my age, so I sought out more adult players. I found three men at Belridge who would accept my challenge. Two were single men who lived in the bunk-house, Ralph and Carl; I loved to play with both men. They were my good friends and were good tennis players. The third person was a man named Charles, he was an older man married with a family: two boys and a girl. His daughter was only a few years younger than I was, and they all lived in one of the company houses. Charles was a Civil Engineer for Belridge Oil Company, was a licensed Civil Engineer, licensed Land Surveyor, and a graduate of Stanford University. He had been my mentor for several years, and started playing tennis with me when I started high school. He encouraged me to play tennis, as well as giving me a few instructions on how to make different shots. I always thought he felt that I had the potential to be a good player. He also helped me set up my curriculum in high school with subjects that would prepare me for future engineering study.

When I got off the bus I raced home and called Charles to see if he was free to play tennis on Saturday morning. He was, so we had a great game the next day. While sitting on the court bench cooling off after the game, he asked about my future plans as I knew he would. I told him that I was at a total loss as to what to do, and that I had no idea which way to turn. Charles's reply was, "Why don't you meet me in my office Monday afternoon, and let's see if we can't work something out for you". So

James William Huckaby
"Mr. Huck"

I did.

I left Charles' office with a lot of new goals: first I would plan to spend two years at Taft Junior College, and get all the classes that the major colleges had to offer. Second I would spend a great deal more time on my tennis. Through all my High School years I had only one hour a day for practice, because I had to catch the bus home. If I missed the bus I had to hitch-hike home and that was very difficult, but I did it many times. If I could get into the college dormitory I would have much more time to work towards a Tennis Scholarship. Charles also got Belridge Oil to give me a summer job working on his survey crew. I left his office with dreams of becoming a great Civil Engineer, working in the oil fields of South America.

The summer came and went, I learned a lot about surveying on Charles' survey crew, and had a few bucks in my pocket. The next thing I needed to do was to get out to Mid-State Petroleum and see if I could get my week-end job back. Gern, (that was a nick-name), was the Boss out there, I never did know his real name. He was glad to see me and said for me to start next Saturday. He said, "Check all the wells when you get here, number 17 may need a bump. She is trying to sand up on us getting only about a half a stroke. Maybe on Sunday you can flood old number eight. I'll see you in the afternoon." The wells pump a certain amount of salt water with the oil into a tank. The water settles on the bottom with the oil on top. The company had a pump mounted on Model A Ford body, powered by the Ford motor that made the pump run. We hooked it up to the tank and pumped the water back into the well. They felt that pumping the water back stimulated the well into

39

producing more oil. Who knows if it worked, but flooding old number eight created a job for me.

I had just finished the hook-up when Bob, the youngest of the three men who worked for Mid State, drove up and jumped out of his car and yelled, "THE JAPS JUST BOMBED THE HELL OUT OF PEARL HARBOR!" "Where is Pearl Harbor" I ask? "I don't know," he said.

It was Dec. 7, 1941.

The following Monday President Roosevelt declared War on Japan, and George and I are headed for the bus stop to go back to college. George has been my friend for years, he lived next door and we went all through high school together. As we get on the bus, Buzz the driver yells, "Not you two again, I thought I got rid of you guys". Buzz is a good friend in fact he stood up with me at my wedding a few months later.

Buzz the bus driver
George was interested in the dormitory too because he

wanted to make the baseball team. So the first thing we did was head for the deans office. He said there was a room available that we could share, and he said we could call it a half athletic scholarship. We were now ALPHA NU EPSILON members (the name of the dorm), which means we got a free breakfast (hot and cold cereal, toast, prunes, and coffee). I would work one hour a day in Miss Pete's high school library for a free lunch. About a block from the campus is a boarding house that serves a home cooked dinner for 50 cents. I can go to town to the bowling alley and set pens and make 50 cents for the next nights' meal.

I signed up for classes in Physics, Surveying, Calculus, and advanced Drawing. I went to the tennis court and found Coach Lee there. He was my high school coach and would also be the college coach this year. I liked Mr. Lee as I felt I had learned a lot from him in four years. I started playing tennis the next day.

Three months have passed and our tennis team is facing a tournament in the town of Ojai. Ojai is about forty miles southeast of Santa Barbara and is well known for their tennis. We were there two days, did fair, but not our best, and ended up with some very severe workouts on our return home. A few more weeks down the road we were sad to hear that the Ojai tournament would be our last and only tournament of the year. All athletic bus trips had been canceled because of the gasoline shortage. A few more months down the road we were sad to here that the high school basketball coach had been drafted, and Mr. Lee would be the new basketball coach; and we would no longer have a tennis coach.

Our tennis program had been cut, but we players would

continue to keep our workouts going. Looks like my athletic tennis scholarship to a larger college just went down the drain. Not just tennis but a short time later all sports would come to a halt. Buses would no longer be used for sports, and only used for transporting students back and forth to school. The country soon got acquainted with rationing. Families were issued War Ration Books: Red Stamps rationed meats, butter, fat, and oil, Blue Stamps rationed canned goods, bottled and frozen fruits. Clothing, shoes, coffee, gasoline, tires and fuel oil were also rationed. Rationing of gasoline and tires depended on the distance of one's job. The specified speed limit was 35 mph, and night time driving was almost completely stopped. Recycling was encouraged and this rationing did not end until 1946.

Somewhere during this period, President Roosevelt ask for a new Selective Service Act that made men between 18 and 45 eligible for military service and were required to register. George and I were in this group so we went to Shafter to do so. I am told that over 10 million men were inducted under this plan.

Everything went as planned the rest of the year as I received passing grades in all my classes. Calculus proved a little rough for me, but I made it. George and I were both working at our sports and were allowed to keep our room at the dormitory for another year. I spent the summer working for Mid-State again and Gern was happy to put me on full time. September I registered for my second year of college, with another year of Calculus, Surveying, Drawing, and I substituted a class of Geology for a class of Physics; a GREAT MISTAKE as I would find out later.

On October 8, 1942 all of the Military Services visited the college with a new enlistment program that allowed all the students who joined that day to remain in school as long as they had passing grades. This sounded great to me, and that very day I was sworn into the United States Navy.

OFFICE OF DIRECTOR
NAVAL OFFICER PROCUREMENT
U.S. NAVAL RESERVE ARMORY
850 Lilac Terrace, Los Angeles, California

October 8,   1940.

From: Director, Naval Officer Procurement.
To: HUCKABY, James William, 412-87-59, AS. V-1(G) USNR.

Subject: ORDERS.

    1.   You have this date been enlisted in Class V-1, U. S. Naval Reserve, for a period of four (4) years, or for the duration of the National Emergency if it exceeds four (4) years. You are directed to proceed to your home on inactive duty and continue in school, subject to call when ordered by The Chief of Naval Personnel or your immediate commanding officer, Commandant Eleventh Naval District, San Diego, California.

    2.   You will keep the Commandant Eleventh Naval District informed at all times of your correct home address.

    3.   You will not leave the continental limits of the United States without first obtaining permission from the Commandant Eleventh Naval District.

                        I. C. JOHNSON,

                        MILO V. OLSON,
                        By direction.

Enlistment Orders

Three days later I received a letter from the Draft Board to report for induction into the United States Army, but they couldn't touch me, because I had already enlisted in the Navy.

I was working on Sunday at Mid-State and my friend Bob come by to talk. He said that General Petroleum was drilling at a new well location about a mile away and that the driller was crying for workers. He said he had helped with a couple of shifts and thought that I might get in a little work there if I wanted it.

I went over that afternoon to see the driller, and he hired me on for the four to twelve shift. I proved that I could handle the work on the floor so he asked when could I go to work for him. I said that I wanted to keep my week-end work at Mid State, but I could take two, possibly three of the afternoon shifts. That meant eight hours on Friday sixteen hours on Saturday and sixteen hours on Sunday. A lot of work that I did for two months and my school work suffered. I ended the quarter failing Geology, and the Navy called me into active duty about three weeks later.

The weeks I spent in Boot Camp in San Diego made me wish I had not flunked Geology. They made a man out of me real quick. I learned how to do my own laundry, using a brush that was part of my new sea bag of goodies. When I reported into the San Diego Training Station I had a little time with the Almighty and said, "God I will not ask for anything special, but will depend on you to point me in the right direction." That was the attitude I approached for my military training.

Near the end of our basic training, they marched us into a big building, sat us down, and gave us each a piece of paper. They asked us to write down three navy "schools" we would be interested in going to. I said, "Lord this wasn't my idea." so I put down three schools, and said, "Aye, Aye, Sir." Later when the school assignments were posted and I checked the long list of names, I finally saw one person assigned to Radar School – that was me. I went immediately to the Chief who was in charge of us and asked him, "What was radar school?" He said he didn't really know about it, but understood that it was a good "rate". I spent the next 6 weeks at Radar School, and quickly discovered it wasn't much of a school: there was very little printed information, and we learned by using the radar equipment they had set up there. They put me in a room with three radar machines, and instructed me to "learn how to use these". From there I went to a receiving station to wait for further orders, with an emblem on my sleeve that said I was a radar operator.

One evening I was reading, and a Lieutenant came in and said he needed 50 men to help unload a ship load of wounded men. We went to the dock and started helping men with all kinds of problems into the aid station for further medical attention. Heart breaking!! Then the Lieutenant said, "Now make two lines about 20 feet apart from the ship to the building. Next will come men with mental problems. You are not to touch them unless some one starts to run". I didn't think I would ever forget the look in the eyes of some of those men. Not a good job for a man waiting assignment to sea duty. It was a bit hard to go to sleep that night.

My orders finally arrived and they read, "You are ordered to take an army troop train to Vallejo, California, and report to the U.S.S. LeHardy, D.E.20. for further duty." The "D.E. stands for Destroyer Escort, and the LeHardy would be my home for the next 3 years. The D.E. 20 was 300 feet long and 30 feet wide, so believe me she was no Cruise Liner. She was more like a large cork that floats on the ocean: bobbing up and down, jumping out of the water, and coming down with a big splash. She would rock right and left past 45 degrees; your chair slides from your radar station into the bulkhead, and you would wonder if she will upright or go on over. She was a hell of a ride if one was prone to sea-sickness, and believe me I was prone sea-sickness. I carried a piece of 3 inch shell casing about 6 inches high that would hold what I would throw up in a 4 hour watch. After my shift I would dump it over the side of the ship on my way aft to my bunk. My body would jump and rock and roll and leap for the next 8 hours trying to sleep. The ship's main duties were to search the water ahead of a convoy for enemy submarines. We had three 3 inch guns, several anti-aircraft guns, depth charges that rolled off or shot out the sides, and hedge hogs (a small depth charge) that shot out over our bow. The LeHardy also had a ramming bow that would cut a submarine in half if it surfaced.

U.S.S. LeHardy, DE-20

After "Shakedown" (preparing the ship for sea duty) the LeHardy was assigned to the "Pineapple Run", which meant escorting convoys of six or eight bigger ships from the west coast of the United States to Pearl Harbor. She sailed on her first cruise to Hawaii on July 21, 1943, and then made two additional runs with convoys before being ordered to remain at Hawaii in late October.

Following training exercises, LeHardy departed Pearl Harbor on November 15th with an Army task force headed for Makin Atoll in the Gilbert Islands. At the same time a Marine task force left New Zealand headed for the Tarawa Atoll in the Gilbert Islands. The Army met little resistance in securing the Makin Atoll (a Japanese Submarine Base). However, Tarawa was different for the Marines, in the 72 hours it took to secure the atoll over 3000 marines lost their lives. Ten days later we continued patrol sub-hunting operations with the 5th Fleet in the vicinity of the Gilbert Islands.

When I first found out what we would be involved in, I got down on my knees and asked God if He would watch over me and let me return to my wife of less than 2 months, I would promise to love her the rest of my life. He kept his side of the deal, and 70 years later I am still working to fulfill my end of the deal. The LeHardy remained off the Gilberts as the U.S. Marines secured the islands, from which the Marshall Islands operation would be launched.

Departing Makin on December 25, 1943, she steamed back to Hawaii for invasion training in preparation for her next assignment. Sailing from Pearl Harbor again on January 28, 1944, the LeHardy formed part of the escort screen for the convoy to the Marshall Islands. She arrived off Kwajalein on February 5th, the day the atoll was secured, and then escorted cargo ships to Funafuti, Ellice Islands. She returned to the Marshalls in mid-

February for patrols and screening duties during the capture of Eniwetok (a 5 day amphibious operation), before sailing for Pearl Harbor on March 4th.

Before the attack on Pearl Harbor, the Kwajalein Atoll was the administrative center for the Japanese 6th fleet whose task was defense of the Marshall Islands. The battle in the Marshalls caused irreparable damage to the Japanese bases. The Japanese island population suffered from injuries and lack of food, with half of the garrison of 5100 people dying from hunger.

Upon our arrival at Pearl Harbor on the Jan 11, 1944, the destroyer escort was assigned to training exercises with the fleet submarines. LeHardy continued these operations until she departed Pearl Harbor late in May, again for operations in the Marshalls. Throughout the summer, we alternated between duties in the western Pacific, and training exercises out of Hawaii.

The Navy about this time converted some of their old Cruisers into flat topped aircraft carriers. One of our training exercises was to accompany one of these ships when the pilots were practicing landing on these short runways. Occasionally one would miss the cable to stop his plane and end up in the ocean. Our job was to rescue the pilot when he surfaced, rig up lines to get him into a boatswain's chair, and send him back to the carrier. In most occasions the Captain of the carrier would send the chair back with ten gallons of ice cream in the chair! If I remember right we saved three different pilots on this duty; thirty gallons of ice cream!
The second exercise was working with the fleet submarines. We would go to sea with a submarine, and they would practice firing dummy torpedoes at our ship.

The torpedoes would be set at depth that would pass right under our hull. One day one of the torpedoes went crazy and plowed right into our ship. I was asleep in my bunk when I awoke to the big bang, and then heard our Captain yell, "It hit at the aft engine room, see how big of a hole it made." It didn't take but a second to hop out of my bunk and get on the main deck. There was no hole but it did split a seam in the hull, and we spent a week in dry dock getting it welded up again. These two exercises were good duty assignments because they required only 2/3rds of the crew on board. The other 1/3rd got liberty in Honolulu.

Another pleasure was that the Navy took over the Great Royal Hawaiian Hotel in Honolulu for their submarine personnel. After the accident they allowed some of us to spend a night there. I had a great time, and their soft beds were not to bad.

From October 22, 1944 until January 22, 1945, Le Hardy escorted tanker convoys from Eniwetok to Ulithi. Sometime in December of 1944 was one of those beautiful warm days you find only in the South Pacific. We were cruising along at about 10 knots, ahead of an eight ship tanker convoy. The ocean was smooth and calm (another thing you find only in the South Pacific in December). I had just settled down at the aircraft radar to start my morning watch. About 10:00 am on the aircraft radar a blip showed on the scope. I immediately challenged it with my I.F.F. switch (I.F.F. - identification friend or foe), and received no response – an unidentified aircraft. When I hit this switch it immediately sets off a response from every aircraft or ship in the area that it is a United States asset. The aircraft on my scope did not respond. We reported it to the bridge; its bearing and distance, and no I.F.F. over and over. The plotter plots its course and the plane is closing in on us. At last they call General Quarters. Every man on the ship has a Battle Station, and gets there as fast as he can; all the guns are manned in seconds, but no order from the Captain to open fire.

I move from the radar to the plotting table. The plane disappears from the scope, and I wonder why. I open the hatch and step out on the deck. There, not 50 feet from the ship and about 15 feet off the water is a white airplane with a big red circle on its side. For a few seconds I make eye to eye contact with two Japanese pilots. I thought they looked like they smiled at me, and it may have been true because all our guns were manned but no shots had been fired. If I had a hand gun I could have killed the bastards, both of them, they were so close.

Orrrrrrrrrrrrrrrr could I????

Would I have frozen up just like our Captain did.? I guess I will never know. One of our officers had been trained on Japanese aircraft and had identified the plane as a Japanese Betty; a reconnaissance plane, but still no guns were fired. I quickly got back to my plotting table, and plotted the plane as it turned and left from the same direction it had come from.

Still no orders to open fire.

Secure from General Quarters sounded and we returned to our regular work. Later that afternoon we heard over our voice radio, "They are bombing the Hell out of us." Japanese planes had intercepted the convoy behind us instead of ours. Our Captain had refused to give the order to fire on the enemy, and he remained in his cabin until we got to Ulithi. He then left the ship and never returned.

It was believed that these Japanese airplanes were from the island of Truk in the Caroline group. Truk was a main base in the south pacific for the Japanese fleet. In February of 1944, Operation Hailstone was executed by the United States on Truk, and was one of the most important navy battles of the war. The Japanese lost 12 warships, 32 merchant ships, and 249 aircraft.

After two years of sailing around the South Pacific, it was time for our ship to have a two year overhaul. On January 22, 1945, we sailed for Seattle, Washington. We were there about three months, and the winter weather was a shock for all of us. From sleeping in nothing but our shorts for years, to scratching for more clothes to keep us warm was a challenge.

Several months prior, a ship was mistakenly sent to Ulithi with a ship load of foul weather gear. All the ships in the bay were ordered to take on foul weather gear for each man on the ship just so the ship could return to the States empty. We only had enough storage for our regular clothes, so where to keep the new gear was a problem. The solution was found on our next convoy east as all of it went overboard. How great it would have been to keep some of it to wear in Seattle several months later.

All the ships engines and generators were rebuilt and looked like new. The only thing that affected us was new radar which was installed for fire control on our big 3 inch guns. Every morning for two weeks I spent ferrying from Seattle to Bremerton to learn how to use the new radar. The radar was put in a small building on the bridge. This was my new station when General Quarters sounded. However the war ended and I never had a chance to use it. Our destroyer escort returned to Eniwetok with a stop-over in San Diego on the way. On May 28th she resumed her Eniwetok-Ulithi convoy runs; her task for the rest of the war. I might add, with the exception of a couple tropical typhoons, the water on the Strait of Juan de Fuca out of Seattle was the roughest I ever experienced. I was seasick before we hit the ocean and remained sick for the six long days it took to get to San Diego.

The Japanese surrendered on August 15, 1945, and signed surrender papers in Japan on September 2, 1945.

LeHardy's Position when the Japanese surrendered
That same day we left Kwajalein in route to Wake Island for surrender ceremonies. The Lehardy stood by as the Japanese Admiral surrendered the island. Wake Island

was the possession of the United States, and was attacked by the Japanese bombers on December 8, 1941. On December 23rd, the Japanese invasion forces landed on Wake Island. After a fierce 16 day siege, 47 marines and 70 civilians were dead, and the Wake Island Garrison surrendered to the Japanese. The U.S. occasionally raided but never made an all out attack on Wake Island. After returning to Kwajalein with surrender papers, we received orders to proceed to Pearl Harbor, and then San Pedro, California, arriving September 27, 1945. The LeHardy was decommissioned October 25, 1945.

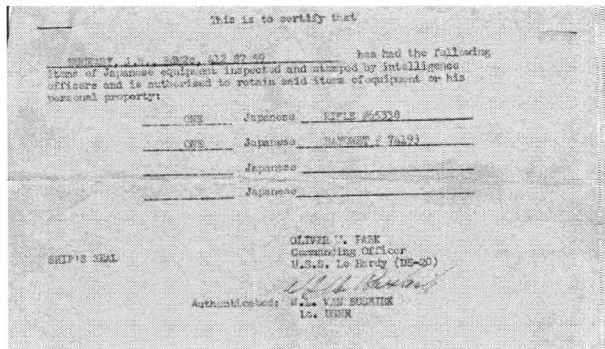

Certification of Japanese Rifle and Bayonet

I enlisted on 10-8-42

I was discharged on 10-14-45

I received $52.51 in back pay and $12.75 travel pay

Initial mustering out pay was $100.00

The thanks I got for three years of my life.

Upon my return, I was devastated to hear that my

mentor and good friend Charles had been killed in an automobile accident while I was away.

The war affected us all.

Chapter Five

THE LADY-BUG, THE LETTER, AND YES, YES!

"If the heavens were open and a Host of angels descended they could not have produced such an effect on my soul as my Mary in her formal dress. The first love is never forgotten.
- Richard Paul Evans

It was late November 1942, my friend George and I were sitting on the high school bus waiting for a ride to Belridge. Two to four times a month we went home from the dorm to get one of our mother's home-cooked dinners. Of course we chose the seat right behind Buzz the driver, so we could tease him. He had a thing going with one of the ladies that worked in the high school office. I watched the other kids board the bus as I knew most all of the ones from Belridge. But WHOA, up stepped a cute little red haired lady-bug I had never seen before. She was dressed in a white blouse, a red plaid mini-mini skirt, white bobby socks, and brown and white saddle shoes. "Buzz, who was that?" I asked.   "I have no idea" he replied. I watched the driver's rear view mirror as she walked back to the middle of the bus.

I occasionally kept my eye on her as the trip went on and boy was she pretty. She remained in her seat during all the stops, and guess what - she got off at our drop-off. I watched as she went walking down the street, and she walked to Don and Marguerite's house. They were a couple about four years younger than me (I was in my second year of college) who married at a very young age. Don's father also worked for Belridge for many years, while Marguerite's father worked for another near by Oil Company. Both had grown up going to the same school we did.

Well, at least I knew where the Lady Bug landed. What to do now?

After eating one of mom's great dinners, I went over to Georges' to hang out. George just lived next door so it was the normal thing to do. All of a sudden a knock on the door brought us to attention. It was Don who came over to invite George to his house to meet Mary. He saw me there too, so I got the invite as well. We had a great evening. After a short stay, George decided to go home. George wasn't to keen on making girlfriends, since they would cost him a coin or two. Like his mother he was tight with his coins. Mary made some chocolate fudge that none of us could eat; it was hard as a rock. The four of us took a nice walk through the camp and before I knew it, Mary and I were walking along hand-in-hand looking at each other with stars in our eyes. Before I left that night, I had Mary's home address in Taft (about thirty miles away) and a date with her to my college Mid-Winter Ball.

Mid-Winter Ball Invitation

I went home walking on air, and dreaming of someone very special in my life. I loved that red hair.

Mary and I had about three weeks to wait for the Ball so we just spent a lot of time together. Mary couldn't throw the dirty dishwater out the door because she would find me standing on her porch. We both still had school to finish, and I knew that there was a future letter coming for me telling me to report to the Navy; and when it would come it would take me away from Mary. So the old saying 'MAKE HAY WHILE THE SUN SHINES' was my first thought. My uncle worked for a gasoline refinery, and a couple of times Mary and I would go out and make the thirty foot climb up the side of the tank to gauge the oil. He had about ten tanks to check, and what a great place to take a girl that you are trying to impress. I could have taken her out to climb one of the old wooden oil derricks, but she probably had done that as a child. That was one of the 'DARING THINGS' every kid had to do before he was accepted into the gang (of neighborhood kids).

About mid-way through the three weeks of dating and waiting, I decided it was time to take Mary out to meet my folks. I think that my mother fell in love with Mary just as fast as I had. I could see she had that, "She will make you a good wife" look in her eyes; Moms start thinking about these things when their son's approach twenty-one.

The Ball was getting closer, and it was time to ask my friends to borrow a suit that would fit me. My good friend Ed, who worked at Mid State, had one that fit like a glove. He said he would let me use it for a fee: I had to work the following Friday for him. I recognized a good deal and took the suit to have it cleaned and pressed. I also bought a shirt with a matching tie, and got permission to use Dads' 41 Chevy (It was much nicer than my 37 Chevy Coupe). Boy was I ready to boogie with the nicest girl in town! Mary looked gorgeous; words can not express how beautiful she was, and boy was I proud to show her off to the crowd.

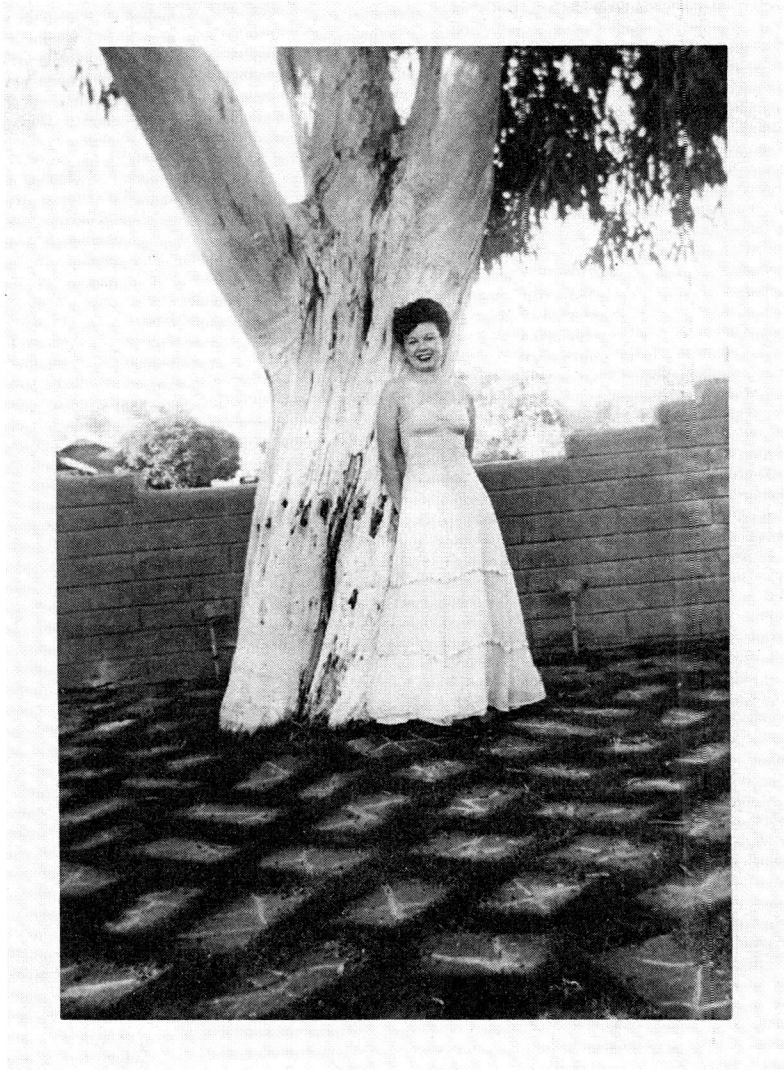

My Mary

I was college class president that year, so the Dean and
his wife, and Mary and I, were in the receiving line.
Everyone who came that night got to meet my Mary. I
hoped that this would help Mary know how I truly wanted
a place in her life in the future. We had a wonderful time

and I hated to see the last song played.

I took Mary out for Chinese food after the Ball; not because the Chinese joint was such a great place but, because it was where all the other guys took their dates. After all, the city of Taft was nothing more than a wide spot in the road. It was either Chinese or the Drive-In for a root beer float. Once inside, you were supposed to carve your initials with a heart around them on one of their tea pots while you waited for your Chow Mein. After dinner, I dropped her off in Taft. I don't remember if I stayed at my dorm in Taft, or if I drove the 30 miles to Belridge; I did it all while I was dreaming. I had to get Dad's car back so it must have been quite a dream.

A few days later, it happened as I had expected, an official summons instructed me to report to the San Diego Navel Training Station for active duty. With only a little over three weeks before my departure, I had to convince Mary that I was worth waiting for. All that was left to keep the spark going was a letter every day, and I wasn't sure that was good enough, but I would try.

James William Huckaby
"Mr. Huck"

Typical Boot Camp Letter

During the three months of training and radar school, my folks made about three trips to see me in San Diego - and they always brought Mary along. On the third trip, my mother got me in a corner and she said, "Don't you treat Mary the way you have treated other girls; she loves you." It wasn't like I had gone through all the girls in the neighborhood. During High School and College I had three girlfriends, and if the truth be told, they all had dumped me. However, I took my mothers' good advice and that night I asked Mary to marry me.

SHE SAID YES!

I offered her the $100 ring I had bought at the PX to seal the deal. Naval pay was not that great, but I could see Mary showing off that ring to every one of her friends.

Skip forward a few months.
I am now on board the U.S.S. LeHardy. We have made two trips to Pearl Harbor, and have just returned to Treasure Island in San Francisco to await another convoy to go back to Pearl. I am standing in line at Western Union with a seven-day pass in one hand while writing out a telegram with the other.

"Mary got seven days leave [stop]
Lets get married [stop]
See you tonight [stop]".

I hopped on a bus that took me right to South Belridge. Mary met me at the bus stop, I borrowed Dads' 41 Chevy and we headed for Taft. First stop was Gardner Field Army Air Force Training Base where Mary worked. She turned in her immediate resignation to insure she would have the whole seven days to spend together. Next was to locate my uncle who was a minister that happened to be holding Revival Services at a church in Taft to marry us. Then I found my friend Buzz, the school bus driver, and told him I needed a Best Man. His reply was. "Have you lost all your marbles doing something as crazy as that?" (He and Annie would get married only a few months later.) With half of the wedding party in tact, next we informed Mary's' parents about the wedding, and then told Mary's sister Betty that we needed a Maid of Honor to complete the ensemble.

Mary and I then headed for Bakersfield to get our blood tests and our Marriage License. Oops, the blood test would take 24 hours - could they put a rush on it? Nope, they wouldn't be ready until noon the next day. We shopped for Mary's wedding dress which turned out to be a cute little blue suit that was good for traveling. We went to a jewelry store where I knew my father had an account, and charged a very modest bill for a wedding ring.

We left Bakersfield at noon the next day for Belridge with everything we needed. We arrived home at about 2:00 pm and told my mother (for the first time) that a task-force from Taft was arriving at 6:30 pm for our WEDDING! Her first reaction was,

"How can this be? I don't have time to clean this house or cook anything."

My mother was ready to kill me, but she had loved Mary since the first time she met her, so that made it ok. When I told my little sister Lois, I thought she would burst with excitement because she knew her brother's new wife would have lipstick, perfume, and jewelry that she could get in to. One of Moms' good neighbors said she would bake up a batch of coconut macaroon cookies to pass around after the wedding.

All arrived at 6:30 pm according to plan - all that is except my Father. That afternoon he had been sent with his truck and trailer to Taft to pick up a load of drill pipe, and then get it back to Belridge. Just to load and tie down a load of 35 foot drill pipe is a time consuming chore.

He finally got home about 8:00 pm.

With the preacher, bride and groom, bridesmaid, best man, five witnesses, plus all the neighbors peeking in the windows, Mary and I promised to love one another the rest of our lives.

Now 71 years later, nuts to those who said it was just a quick war time wedding that would not last.

I thanked my friend Buzz for coming, and true to form he told me, "Those macaroon cookies were the only thing that kept me here waiting for your dad those three hours - boy I loved those cookies." As I recall he had one in his mouth, and one in his hand every time I looked at him.

James William Huckaby
"Mr. Huck"

Our Wedding Picture

We spent our Honeymoon, and the rest of my seven day leave in Belridge. Leave time always passed quickly, and the final day of leave found us on our way to Alameda, CA where Mary's aunt and her Navy husband lived. We were invited to stay there until I shipped out. We were there only eleven short days, and then I shipped out to Pearl Harbor.

It would be 18 months before I would see my new bride again.

Chapter Six

THE FUTURE IN FRESNO

*"I feel as if the fuse has been lit on a bomb
that I am helpless to disarm
Sometimes you can't go home again"*
- Richard Paul Evans

Having just been discharged from the Navy, here it is decision time again - and this is a big one:

Where to work and live the rest of our lives?

The big CEO of Belridge had been by the house no less than three times telling me that he had a job waiting for me when I was ready to go to work. I suppose they would have had a house available for us to live in? I had worked in the oil fields for four years doing a number of jobs, so the work is something that I was familiar with.

I had a good life as a child in Belridge. Having visited my grandma as a child growing up, I knew my way around. I had passed all the "dare you" tests, with my pals, gone all way to the top of a wooden derrick, and walked across a canyon on a jack line. I knew how to chew the tar from the tar vat, and where the camp dump was with all the good stuff people threw away. After my grandmother died in 1935, we moved there from Fresno permanently. It became my home, and I remember riding my bicycle through fields of beautiful wild flowers, the swimming pool in the summer afternoons, the tennis court where all the gang of kids gathered until about 11:00 pm, and the two-teacher school house that had 8 grades. It was in Belridge my parents brought my baby sister Lois home. I saw the car from the playground and then ran to my teacher to see if I could go home and see her. When I got back to school I told my sister Betty she needed to go home and see the new addition.

In my heart I thought that I could be happy at Belridge; but what about Mary? She had always lived in the city of Taft. It wasn't much of a city, but it had a lot of pluses that Belridge did not have.

To confuse the issue even more, my uncle Charlie in Fresno called and said he had a friend who thought he could get me a job at Pacific Gas & Electric; and, if I was interested come as soon as possible. My grandmother, Uncle, and two aunts would be there to help us get settled, and welcome us with open arms. I had hoped I could find something in the field of surveying because that was the area I had the most training. This job with PG&E just might be a better choice for me, and Mary might like Fresno better than being stuck in an oil camp, surrounded by oil derricks in the middle of the desert.

After visiting Ojai and Santa Barbara on the tennis team, I couldn't make a decision with out exploring them as well. I had to see for myself if they might be a possibility for us to make a future home there. Mary and I again borrowed Dads' 41 Chevy, packed a couple of suitcases, and left one morning. We went through Taft and Maricopa, and then drove west across the coast range to Ojai. After much searching we finally found a motel that had a room. We then checked out the town, and the newspapers for rentals and job opportunities. The next day we did the same thing in Santa Barbara. Both cities were beautiful places to live, but both places were way beyond what we could financially afford; not that day or well into the future. So I put away my pride and told Mary that I thought we would be happier down the road somewhere else. The next day we drove north to Pismo Beach, and then continued on to Paso Robles. We spent a little time at the old Mission, then went east on Highway 46.

At the little town of Shandon, CA, Highway 46 joins Highway 41. A little further east is a wide spot in the road called Cholame. It is there that Highways 41 and 46 split apart: highway 46 goes on towards Bakersfield in the direction of Belridge, while highway 41 turns northeast toward Fresno. I stopped the car well out of traffic and said, "Mary it's decision time. The next time I start the car we will know where we will start a new life." I told her it was time to talk and to pray and make sure we both agree on what to do. First, we could go back to Belridge where I know I have a job, and know how to handle the work. We can get a house in the camp, and have our kids go to the same little two teacher schoolhouse that I did. That decision was really not a big challenge, and I would be making the easier choice. Or second, we could take Highway 41 and go to Fresno and take a shot in the dark. I may be able to find a job and stay with relatives until we can find a house. A lot of unknowns, a lot of 'what if's', but we had been separated for 18 months and at least we would be doing it together. After about an hour it was, START THE CAR WE ARE GOING TO FRESNO!!

Because we had Dad's car we had to return it to him, so we turned right on Highway 46 headed for Belridge. We told the folks about our decision; I think they were happy for us, but I also think they would have liked for us to stay there. The first thing we needed was a car, so we found a 1938 Chevy coupe for sale. Dad and I went to look at it and decided it would do the job for us. Even used cars were hard to find that soon after the war. We loaded everything we owned (which wasn't much), into the back end of the car and headed off into the future.

Mothers' youngest sister Irene and her husband Frank welcomed us with open arms. They offered us a bedroom that we shared with their young son Franklin. Tight quarters for sure, but we were glad to have their friendship and love. Apartments or houses for rent were totally non-existent as there was never anything listed in the paper. My grandmother helped out some by letting us use her little apartment while she visited a friend for two weeks.

I sought out my Uncle Charles' friend at PG&E and it went just as he had said. I then had an interview with Glenn, the man who was in charge of the surveying department. He said he still had three surveyors that hadn't come home from the war yet, and he had to save their jobs for them when they got out. He told me if I wanted to take the chance one of the men wouldn't come back for his job, I could take one of the vacant positions. We agreed that I would work on a survey crew for two weeks to learn their procedures. While waiting to be oriented on one of their crews, I worked in the back room trimming maps when they came out of the printer. Two weeks later, having never gone out on a crew, Glenn came into the back room and asked, "Are you ready to take out a crew now?" He needed a crew in the field the next Monday, and this was Friday; that was the beginning of a great relationship with Glenn. He trained me to the point that I was doing the most important jobs that came across his desk. Eleven years later, I would take and pass the test for the State of California Licensed Land Surveyor; I was now James William Huckaby, L.L.S. In later years, I replaced Glen upon his retirement as head of the surveying department.

Having just been given the job with PG&E, I then received a phone call from my uncle John who said that a friend of his had a room for rent. It was in a big old two story house that had a small room upstairs with a cooking area. Mary and I went and checked it out. The furnished room had a sofa that opened out to make a bed, a table with a couple of chairs, and a bathroom that we shared with an elderly couple next door. They had a room just like ours with the addition of a bedroom. We jumped at the deal and moved right in with our meager belongings. At last, a home of our own for two crazy kids. We stayed there for several months until the people next door moved out, so we took their set up with the extra bedroom. It was here where our little Connie Lou was born.

The Landlord also had a small home located behind the big house that became available. So we moved from the one bedroom into the small house and stayed there several months. We became pretty adept at moving since we didn't have much to move and had a lot of practice.

A year later (1954) I received another call from my uncle John. This was somewhat of a surprise as I had not seen him in awhile. He said that a man he worked with lived out in the country a little ways in a small group of houses, and one of them was up for sale. He thought that I could buy it for about $3,500 dollars, so we went out to look at it along with my uncle. It was a small house on a very large lot with two bedrooms, living room, kitchen, bathroom, and a small wash area for laundry. It had its own well and a lot of area for a garden. It was a diamond in the rough; all we could see was house space, land space, and open country air. We went to the Veterans Office to get a G.I. Loan, and moved in as soon as it was approved.

Our Country Home

This was our land, and one day I would own it free and clear. I learned that $3,500 dollars was a lot of money in those days; but I had fun earning it. The first thing I did was build a fence all around the property, and then built Mary a clothes line to hang up towels and sheets. Next was to spade up all that land on the east side of the house and plant a huge garden. I planted every kind of vegetable I could think of, along with every kind of weed there was in the neighborhood. Work, work, work, but think of the goodies that would come out of our garden. The neighbors behind us raised chickens and sold their eggs for a little extra income. Good idea! I had lots of room in the back that I could build some chicken coops to raise some chickens. A few trips to the lumber yard, a slab of cement, some hammering and sawing, and finally a woven wire fence around it; I was all set. My next door neighbor suggested we should go together and buy fifty little chicks to raise some chicken fryers; sounded good to me. The people behind me loaned me a chicken brooder to keep the chicks warm, and all I had to do was get electricity to it; then we were off to get our fifty chicks. I don't remember how many fryers we ended up with but he took his share and I took mine to the place that killed, dressed, and kept them in a freezer for us. I think that we could have bought them at the store for much less than all this cost.

Meanwhile, everything was growing in my garden. I found out that my well was more for domestic use and not to irrigate a small farm. I had to have the pump company come out and lower the pump so it would be below the water line. The peas, carrots, corn, radishes, lettuce, and the one good watermelon that the squirrels ate, I could have purchased at the fruit stand for much less than what the pump man charged me.

I ended up hiring two men to clean and level the land, and then plant it all into grass; I was out of the farming business.

Well, with grass to mow and an empty chicken coop, I thought that was a good time to bring my horse "Honey" to town. She could nibble on the grass and stay in the chicken pen. When Mary's folks bought their little farm in the Centerville area, they had two horses that went with the place. I bought one of them from the folks and kept her out on their farm. A neighbor had a horse that was broke to ride, and he would trade for mine that was not yet broken. I said yes and that was how I got Honey. So I thought she could take the place of pulling weeds. I quickly discovered that Honey was a little large for the chicken pen and that she needed more than a nibble or two of grass to eat. Dad asked to take Honey on a deer hunting trip and then to Belridge where he would build her a nice pasture.

That sounded like a deal to me and I went out and bought a lawn mower instead.

Another thing we discovered early on after we bought the place was that the builder did a very poor job on the septic system. My father and I ended up replacing the entire system. It became obvious to me that my father truly loved me to join me in this project.

Not everything in our country home was bad; in May of 1955 God blessed us with the birth of our second child: a beautiful little baby girl we named Carol Ann.

A few months later I decided to throw in the towel on country living. Mary and I (mainly Mary) agreed that I was truly a city boy at heart and should give up on the rural life. We put the house up for sale, and when it sold we moved back into Fresno and rented a house for about a year.

We were well into the summer of 1957 when I was returning from working on a building project (you will read about later) with dad up at Huntington Lake late Sunday night. My Mary caught me as I was stepping out of the car and said, "Stop! You've got to see the house I found!!" We tucked Connie and Carol into the car, and quickly drove to 3045 North Farris Avenue; and there sat the house where we would spend the next fifty-three years of our lives.

We called the Realtor, and even though it was late, she agreed to show us the inside. The house was next to an elementary school which was a God-send. Carol could walk to school saving Mary from having to load up Connie every day to drive her to and from school. We agreed with the owner's price of $10,500 dollars, and then applied for a California Veteran's Loan that faced one problem: it would take one year for the loan to go through. The owners agreed to wait for their money and rent the house to us for $57 a month. Papers were signed, one year later to the day the owners got their money, and we were the new owners of the house at 3045 North Farris Avenue; our home. We quickly got used to the sounds of children playing and the school bell going off every hour during the school year. Once some rambunctious boys got the idea to tie our dog's ears to the fence; he was no worse for wear.

There are tons of other things I could write about our fifty-three years there; but, since the winter of my life is closing in very rapidly, we should move along with the rest of the story.

We sold the house in Fresno in September of 2009 and moved two hours north to the Vintage Independent Retirement Living in Lodi, CA to be near our son Bill, his wife Cathy, and their family. It was a temporary move of only eighteen months as we ended up buying another home in Lodi; right across the street from an elementary school. We had come full circle.

We will remain here until we make our final move to that home our Father in Heaven has prepared for us. Mary and I will be there to welcome you to our first Bible study. See you there.

Chapter Seven

THE GREAT P.G. & E.

*"We spend our lives building higher fences and stronger
locks. When the gravest dangers are already inside.
A little spark kindles a great fire."*
- Paul Evans

After the hard-learned lesson of the Battle of Tarawa, the
United States launched a successful air and land assault
on Kwajalein and Eniwetak Atolls on February 3, 1944.
The two Atolls served as advanced air and navel bases,
as well as safe place through which to advance the
supply lines. On August 15, 1945, the USS LeHardy
was at anchor on the Kwajalein Atoll, when over the loud
speaker we heard this, "Now hear this: just in on the
telegraph wire,

"THE JAPANESE HAVE SURRENDERED. THE WAR
IS OVER!"

The ship's crew went wild; we could not believe it. For
three years we had waited to hear those words, and yet
it was still a total shock.

My first thoughts were, "How soon do I get off this ship
and out of this Navy?" My answer would have to come
from Mike, Yeoman First Class who kept track of all of
the records. Mike's office was one deck below the radar
compartment, right beside the ladder that took us up to
our watches. I said, "Mike tell me how soon I can think
about discharge." He pulled my records and answered,
"Well, you signed up for four years, you will get out on
October 8, 1946." That meant another year and fifty-four

days to go. "SHOW ME", I asked. There it was in black and white, United States Naval Reserve 10-8-42 for four years; 10-8-46 seemed like a lot more than four years.

Two weeks later, Mike told me that he had received notice that members of the Reserve would be discharged just like everyone else when they had the proper amount of points. We earned points for a number of things: Time in the service, where it was spent, and extra time in the war zone, etc. But the biggie was an extra ten points awarded to married men. Mary's ten points popped me over the top. When the USS LeHardy docked in San Pedro Bay on October 27, 1945, and the gang plank was down, I was the second one off the ship headed for the Discharge Center. Exactly 73 days after the Japanese surrendered, I was a civilian!

Mary and I had talked a lot about my returning back to school. There were some good offers to veterans who wanted further education, but for me it would take several years of college. We decided that with several million veterans coming out of the service maybe the best thing to do was to find a good job first, and later take a few Junior Colleges classes.

I have previously written about how I had acquired a job at Pacific Gas & Electric working for a fine man named Glen. He taught classes on surveying at Fresno City College which I took. He encouraged me to get my Land Surveyors License from the State of California's Board of Registration for Civil Engineers and Land Surveyors. He was licensed both as a Civil Engineer and a Land Surveyor. He gave me several books to get me started and I studied for about six years both at home and in the office at night. In early 1953, I decided to take the two-day test given by the State Board. As I expected, I failed the test and had go back to square one. I did however get some very good ideas of what I needed to study more. In the summer of 1955 I took an entire month of vacation at the camp at Huntington Lake in concentrated study. Later in 1955 I took the test again and passed the written portion, but the Board wanted me to take an oral test as well and would notify me as to the date of the test.

At this time, I heard a rumor that the State of California Department of Parks and Beaches was giving a test for surveyors to work for them. One of the requirements was the surveyor must have a state license. Knowing I was kind of in a limbo with my oral, I decided to take their test also. I got a letter that I had passed, and to report to San Francisco for an oral test. About three days later, I got a job offer from the Department of Parks and Beaches, and the next day another job offer from somewhere in Sacramento came in. Well don't you know I took those two letters in and laid them on Glen's desk and said, "Glen, I'm going to take one or the other of these jobs, or I want more money to stay at P.G.&E.". "Leave the letters and go to work" he replied. The next morning when I came in, Glen handed me a slip of paper saying my title was changed from Surveyor to Senior Surveyor with a substantial raise. I was glad that Glen fell for my bluff because I could not have taken either job since I was still waiting to take my oral test with the State of California for my license. After months and several letters, the board said they had reviewed my written test and I would not need to take the oral test and I received my license shortly after.

Now with my license, I could go into private practice and

I had an offer from a private Surveying firm in Fresno. Up until now I had never done any outside work from P.G.&E., but I told this firm I would do some side jobs for them on the weekends if they needed me. I respected the private surveyors and would recommend them if I was approached to do outside work. They respected me for sticking with my P.G.&E. work, and leaving the private work for them. As a result, their offices were always open to me for any information that I needed. This was a great asset to me in my work, and I was always open to them if we had any information they needed.

By June of 1946, I had worked for Glen at P.G.&E. for about eight months when he told me he wanted my crew to meet him at the Bass Lake Dam at 8:00am the next day. He said that I should bring a change of old clothes. I wasn't sure I could even find Bass Lake as most of my work had been around Fresno. We all arrived at the appointed time and in a few minutes a hydro crew arrived. The crew foreman was named Wally. On the dam was a huge tripod and laying flat on the ground under the tripod were two huge metal doors. Wally took a key and opened the doors, revealing a huge four foot shaft going down into the dam. Wally says to Glen, "We got the pump in yesterday and pumped it down but the pump lost its prime and we had to do it several times, and I hope we can get it working today."

Glen then tells me, "This shaft is 150 feet deep, with a brass pin set in the cement every five feet all the way to the bottom. At the bottom is a two-inch brass pin that will be covered with muck that Wally will have to find. The shaft is tilted, and you will need to take a measurement every five feet using a plumb bob and a four foot ruler as you are descending on the ladder, and then shout out the readings. Be sure to hang on to the ladder all the time!!!" There was no safety line.

However, the bottom twelve feet of the shaft was full of water which means three pins were under water. Now Wally was down at the bottom of the shaft, and he started the pump to get that water out of there. Glen then told me, "Try and get the measurement on the two pins at the bottom when the water gets down to about three feet. Wally will find the pin in the bottom and work the suction hose around it. The minute the hose pump sucks air, the pump will stop. The water will rush in and you have less than a minute to get your reading. ARE YOU READY? LET'S GO." I was terrified, but I wanted to keep my job. I didn't realize that I would repeat this job every year for the next 36 years since I was one of the few people who wasn't bothered by the close quarters of that four foot shaft. I never felt comfortable asking anyone else to do it, so over the years Wally and I became very good buddies.

"Lawrence" was the claims adjuster for the P. G. & E. and he could destroy a perfect day for me in about thirty seconds. His job was to collect all the evidence on accidents, whether it was a dent on someone's car, or some one got killed on a power line contact. From his first phone call he was hot to trot. His office was on the 7th floor, and when I saw him coming out of the elevator between a trot and a run on the 5th (where our offices were) it was trouble for someone. If he went to our head draftsman that was good because he needed him to go out with him to measure up and prepare a map for an automobile accident. If he went into Glen's office, I knew that Glen would call me in to survey an electrical accident. I hated these with a passion as they required a greater degree of precision. You had to show every little detail on the power poles that are involved; wire heights, ground elevations, and set monuments that will be there if you have to go back for additional information. The Bass Lake Dam survey is a piece of cake compared to an accident survey. There is always the possibility that you might end up in court.

I did an accident survey years ago in Madera County where a farmer got a metal irrigation pipe up into a power line. The farmer did not get killed, but he was crippled from the electrical contact. About a year later, one morning Glen said that the case was going to court and both attorneys would need me to give a deposition. When I arrived I saw the P. G. & E. attorney was an older gray haired man, dressed in a black suit, white shirt, a tie, and shined shoes.

The opponent attorney was a young man dressed in a coat and slacks. I showed them where the accident happened, the monuments I had established and, answered any questions. They then went to someone's office where our attorney spent the rest of the morning questioning the man who had been injured while his attorney watched and I waited outside.

After lunch it was my turn. Our attorney sat in a chair thumbing through a magazine while the other attorney questioned me. I had my field notes with me, and he asked if he could look at them. I looked at our attorney and he nodded 'yes'. Then he asked if he could keep them to study. That would be a 'no-no' to me, but our attorney said sure. That about ended it all; we all got up shook hands, and our attorney wished the other attorney

good luck in his OTHER cases. Before we left, I
questioned our attorney about the casual attitude he
had, and why he let my notes go. He said. "I got all the
information I need to sew up this case from the injured
party this morning. Nothing you could do or say will
change that." You never know when an old accident
survey will awake to haunt an old surveyor.

In 1948, a job came up working with the Hydro
department in the Bass Lake area. They were going to
replace two wooden flumes with steel ones. These two
flumes ran from the Bass Lake dam above, to a lake
down below. The flumes were built in such a way so as
they would meet in the middle; a real challenge for a
surveyor. My calculations and measurements would
determine whether they lined up when they reached the
middle or not. The construction foreman was full-
blooded Swedish and every body called him "The
Swede." His powder man was a full-blood North Fork
Indian and every one called him "Chief". Part of my
figures had to allocate for a two-inch space to allow for
final adjusting to the proper elevation when the flume
was completed. A year before, one of our surveyors
forgot this two-inch measurement, and they had to blast
out some footings and redo them. Every one on The
Swede's crew would remind me everyday about the two
inches.

I started working with the powder man to get the rocks
blasted out for the footings. I just took one man with me,
and a roll of maps of the two flumes. I went over and
over my calculations every night to make sure I was
right. Well, the steel started going up, and everything
was matching up and fit as it should. The Swede pulled
a fast one on me as right when we were ready to set the

last section of the large flume, he yells, "Lunch time." We go back to Bass Lake and eat lunch. When we get back The Swede put in the missing middle section. It worked perfectly. I said, "Swede you made me sweat out that whole lunch hour wondering if that last section was going to fit in there." He said, "I knew it would fit, I measured it with a rope." All my precise measuring and he used a rope. All my worry was in vain. Well, we graded in both steel flumes, packed up our gear, and thanked all the guys for reminding me all those times about the two inches. I think we spent about six weeks on the entire job. The job had challenged my brain a good bit and I was glad to get back to my regular work.

In 1970 I got a call from Glen on a Sunday night telling me a crop duster had taken out a five hundred thousand KV Power line (our largest line) over in the Coalinga area. He said he needed my crew out there at 7:00am the next morning. When I got there I met Lawrence (my favorite pal) and the tower foreman on the job site. I saw Lawrence excitedly jumping all around the tower men; which was his way. The duster had caught one of the outside power lines in between the two towers and ripped the line from three towers leaving approximately 1300 feet of high voltage line on the ground. About 150 feet away was where the plane burned up and left a fairly large burn area. I asked the foreman what I could do for him first; and he said he was concerned that one leg of the tower footing had been pulled up out of the ground, and would I check that tower and the three towers north. We went right to work and sure enough, the tower footing had pulled up about six inches and one of the others about two inches. The three towers north had no problem. He said he didn't think the six inches would be a problem, but he would have to check and see for sure. He told me to go ahead with my work and he would proceed with trying to get the lines off the ground.

I started by getting a ground profile between the two towers where the power line was hit, and one tower on either side of them. I got the line heights at all four towers with three measurements in between. I tied in the site where the plane ended up and measured up the burn area. Found the nearest section corners and tied them in so the exact location could be related to the accident. Shot the sun for bearing, and took temperature at noon for the three days we were there. Never heard anything more from Lawrence or anyone else on that one!

I had another Hydro job that was a bit difficult for me. The lake feeding the Balch camp powerhouse was filling up with sand that was taking up valuable space that could have been filled with water. The company was going to dredge it out and blow it over to the other side of the dam. A contractor would do the job, but we must determine the amount of sand he removed as he would be paid by that amount. My job was to set the lake up on a twenty-five foot grid system taking soundings every twenty-five feet all over the lake bottom; I had never seen the lake and had no idea how I would attack the job.

I got on the site and discovered the lake to be pear shaped with the dam on the south end of the lake. The lake was about 700 feet long and about 250 feet at its widest part. I figure I needed an additional 500 foot chain and a row boat. I checked with the camp foreman and he said he would have the boat in the lake that day.

I went back to Fresno to pick up the second 500 foot chain from one of the other crews, along with some rope to be ready for the next day. Fortunately the weather was very pleasant so working on the water wasn't that bad. Using the dam as my base line, I went about laying out my grid in twenty-five foot sections. I then put a man on the side of the lake that lined us up with the floats, and stopped us every twenty-five feet to take a sounding. It took rest of the week to complete the job, and we returned the boat and picked up all our tools.

After finishing the job, I went back to work on Monday to blow off some steam. The company had some nice rooms for the workers at Balch Camp, but the hydro crews had all of them occupied. We on the other hand had to use the old overflow building that was filthy: two-foot metal cots with two-inch pads, and dirty showers; the worst I'd ever seen. The only thing that helped was our wonderful cook. She turned out some wonderful food and great lunches. (The cook at Bass Lake, on the flume job, had starved us to death.) That morning talking to Glen I turned the air blue complaining about the place we had to stay and refused to ever stay there again.

Everything went as usual until about mid-December. That year Glen let me have a double cross right on the kisser. The guy running the dredger at Balch needs his money for the amount of sand he has removed so it had to be sounded again. This was not part of the deal as far as I was concerned even though he said it had to do with his taxes. The same men went back with me and we fought the weather all the way through it. Ice formed on the tape as I made the soundings. Most all of the mountain camps have a cottage set up for the big shots when they want to stay overnight or for a weekend. Guess what? That's where we stayed for a week and had a fire in the fireplace every night.

In the spring the dredger was finished, and we needed to take the final soundings so he could get paid. We left on Monday morning and got our chains in place and our boat in the water. We would start Tuesday morning on taking soundings. I was watching TV after dinner (we had the cottage again) when in walked Rodger, one of the men that worked with me. He had a big fifth bottle of whiskey and handed it to me. He said, "It's from the dredger guy. He said that maybe you could add a few extra inches to my sounding readings." "Rodger," I said " take this back to the dredger guy and tell him that he gets what he's got coming not a inch more. Tell him that I cannot be bought." After what he did to me last December I had no sympathy for him.

Because the following was not a P.G.&E project I will give it a title:

The Best Laid Plans Fall Apart

Willard and Gene were partners in a young surveying firm that I did some side jobs for on the weekends when they got behind. Willard was the one that had approached me about going to work for them after I got my license, but I had refused. Their firm got the contract for surveying the New China Peak Ski Resort up near Huntington Lake. So I took a helper and spent a weekend doing some topography work for two parking areas.

A short time later, the firm split up. Willard disappeared,

but Gene kept the firm, the office, the personnel, and the China Peak contract. This job was a kind of an off-and-on project during the winter. One day I was in his office getting some information for a job I had to do, when Gene cornered me and told me that the China Peak project had come alive again, and he had to furnish them with a profile of the ground up to the top of the peak, where the chair lift would be. He asked me if I could get some men to help him the next weekend. I gathered up three men and myself, along with Gene who had all the equipment we needed in his station wagon and off we went. When we arrived, Gene showed us where the lift would start, and up the mountain we went. Gene would be the recorder, I put my regular transit-man on the instrument, and another on the head-end of the chain, and I and another man would cut brush. We finished the job about 5:30pm that day at the top of the mountain. We had all the information that Gene needed for the profile.

It would be dark before we got to the bottom, and normally what I do in that situation is to line all five men up and would go down keeping a space between each man, with the lead man hollering and each man responding the same way. The head man would wait until he heard each man respond. About the second time we did that, Gene did not respond. I stopped the group and went back and found Gene laying face down in the snow. We rolled him over and he made no response. I immediately started artificial respiration on him (CPR hadn't been discovered yet), even though we thought he was dead. One other man knew how to do artificial respiration, and between the two of us we kept it going for six hours. I told one of my men to get a huge fire going. I sent another man down to the car to get the forest ranger, to contact Margaret (who worked for Gene) to tell Gene's wife what had happened, and to contact his own wife and ask her to notify our wives as to what was going on. When he got to the car it had a flat tire he had to change. The two of us continued to work on Gene while Jim kept the fire going.

Finally we saw lights on the road below. The Forest Ranger had notified the men that worked at the Big Creek Power House, and four men from there came up with the Ranger. The Ranger and others said that Gene was dead, but he could not move him without the Coroners' permission. He would go back down and get his permission, and when he got it, he would drive back and blink his lights two times which would mean to bring him down. We saw the Ranger drive back and blink his lights, so we stopped our efforts, and began carrying Gene's body down the hill; it was about 6:00 am the next day. We arrived at Gene's office about 10:00 am and I had a long talk with Margaret. She was Gene's draftsman whom I had known for years; in fact, she worked for Glen before she went to work for Gene. I considered Gene a great friend, but I decided right then I was through helping other people. I would stick to my own work; it was enough of a challenge for me.

These are but a few of my head full of memories. There are many others like a campground survey at Courtright Lake, a road survey from Courtright dam to the trail head, property surveys at Wishon Lake, Los Banos, Atascadero, and Paso Robles, a substation in Fresno, 70 thousand volt lines in Santa Maria, Bakersfield and Coalinga, 110 thousand volt tower line from Herndon to Fresno, a seventeen mile aerial survey in the Sequoia National Forest, plus about a hundred thousand miles of

12 thousand volt distribution line.

Furthermore, cutting brush and poison oak in 114' F temperature was not fun but, at the end of the day what did we accomplish? We chopped 1,000 feet of brush and set two pole locations. That meant that the next day we had two less poles to stake than we had before. This is how I looked at each day after work. What did I accomplish that day?

I had a dear little friend who was less than 5 foot tall. He was a friend of my father. The three of us went on a hunting trip one time. Little Bill was probably about 60 years old and tough as nails. He was an Oil Rig Builder all of his life; he built these wooden oil derricks that were used in the old oil fields. His major tool was what he called a hatchet. He could drive nails with it or chop wood with it. He also used it as a weapon if someone got smart about his height. He told me something around a camp fire one night that I have lived by ever since: "Bud when you get married, you treat your wife like a queen. She is the most precious thing you will ever have. And when you hire out for an eight hour job, you give a full eight hours." So that is kind of how I have tried to live according to little Bill.

Have I enjoyed my jobs and would I do it again? I would say 'yes' - up to the point to where I took over the department. I loved the time I spent in the field with my crew, but I was totally not happy with my desk. I quickly learned that management and workers are not always happy campers. Either one or the other was upset over something.

Do I have any regrets? I think the only ones were the

additional burdens it placed on Mary taking care of three little children when I was working away from home.

This I know, that with all the burdens, my Mary danced with me to and through my retirement. For that, I am eternally grateful.

Chapter Eight

MY ANGEL

*The greatest work you will ever do will be
as a father to your own home. I do not know why we
delude ourselves that life is predictable and safe,
when it's really just a carton of eggs.
Always just one stumble away from being scrambled."
- Richard Paul Evans*

Our Angel Connie

The only communication available to Mary and I during the eighteen months we were separated while I was in the Navy was the mail service; and we kept it very busy. Even when I was in boot camp we would write every day. In the beginning our ship would escort merchant ships and tankers from Pearl Harbor to Eniwetok (in the Marshall Islands), pick-up empty ships, and return them to Pearl. Each trip would take from six to eight days depending on the speed of the convoy. Some of the older ships had problems keeping up with the newer ones. Whether we were coming or going, there was always about six letters waiting for me when we hit port, and I would have some to be mailed back to Mary.

I would sometimes start a letter, then add to it each day, so Mary would end up receiving a six to eight page letter. Later, we would convoy from Eniwetok to Ulithi (in the Caroline Islands) but the distance made no difference; with the mail the six letters were always there. We made all kinds of plans for the future, but the major one was we both wanted to start our family the next time we were together. In January 1945, my ship was ordered to sail to Seattle, WA for a two-year overhaul. Mary and I had almost three months together; we spent that time Belridge, Oregon, and Washington. We danced to the music of the Mid Winter Ball of 1942 because we hoped that we had a baby in the cooker.

The "C" Division (communication division) was made up of radiomen, signalmen, radar and sonar men, and we were responsible to stand watch while we were in port. The radiomen stood their dot and dash watch, the signalmen were on their flags and blinkers, and the radar and sonar men stood the voice radio and gangway watch. Once in the middle of the night while I was on watch, in walked my friend Henry (one of my fellow radar men). He was a tall skinny Texan that lived with his mother and he sent her a good portion of his money. Henry was scheduled to relieve me in about an hour. I asked him why he was not asleep, and he said he couldn't, and had just come up to talk.

We talked a bit and finally he said, "I really want to talk about something I read while I was in Texas on leave." He said "I read an article that said that people exposed to a lot of radar activity could possibly have problems with their reproductive system in the future." He said the article was not conclusive but was more like a warning, and because he knew that I was married, he thought that I should know about it. We talked a little bit more and finally Henry said,"Go hit your sack I'll do the rest of your watch." To this day, I have never repeated Henry's article to anyone; however, I had times in my life when I wondered about it a lot. One of those times was two weeks later when Mary wrote that she was not pregnant and that our plans had not come to pass. I sent a letter back trying to encourage her saying there would be another dance. In my mind, I could not help but wonder about the talk that Henry and I had that night.

About a year after leaving the Navy, we are two happy kids living in our one room apartment. One day I was downstairs trying to clean up the old 38 Chevy coupe and Mary was hanging out the upstairs window talking to me. "WHAT DID YOU JUST SPIT OUT OF YOUR MOUTH?" she asked. The day before my survey crew and I were working staking out about a mile of power line and a tobacco salesman drove by and stopped to talk. He said that he thought we looked like old tobacco chewers and he gave each one of us a cut of Red Man.

Mary yelled down to me, "YOU ARE CHEWING TOBACCO. SPIT THAT OUT, and don't ever do that again if you ever want me to kiss you." To be sure I threw away the rest of the Red Man! By this time my Mary was about five months pregnant and I would never do anything to upset her. It was about this time that the apartment next door became available, and we moved in to get a bedroom. Now Mary had a full size bed to sleep in as her tummy grew, instead of the pull out bed of our studio apartment.

I think that this is a good time to explain the cover of this book. "A LITTLE TO THE RIGHT" was exactly where I should have been with my life. Surely, you know by now that I was a Land Surveyor.

Surveying Power Lines

James William Huckaby
"Mr. Huck"

Over the years I had surveyed many miles of power lines; so why not use the skills that I know to tel a story. The power line, which represents my life, is short to symbolize how young I was at this point in my life. Off to the right stands the Cross of Christ, and notice they are miles apart; that's where I was in my relationship with Jesus at 26 years of age. But I am about to hear the news that would later draw me closer to Him.

Mary's Pregnancy with Connie

On August 24, 1946, I rushed Mary to the hospital as she was ready to deliver. It was a long and hard labor; the delivery was about mid-afternoon when our little daughter Connie Lou was born. She was diagnosed with Cerebral Palsy due to the serious brain damage that occurred during her birth. I couldn't believe it! It wasn't fair, truly it wasn't, but there was nothing I could do to change it.

We took Connie to every doctor we could find, but their only reply would be, "There are hospitals for youngsters like this". Not wanting to accept this we took her to the greatest hospital we could find, the University of San Francisco, for two days of examinations. Their response was the same, "Put her in a Institution and get on with your lives." As a last resort, we took her to a Faith Healer and had her prayed for but nothing changed. Back in Fresno we found a pediatrician who was very kind and gentle, and helped us to keep Connie as healthy as possible. The truth was that Mary kept Connie alive for fourteen years with her constant motherly love. She learned how take care of all of Connie's needs. Connie never talked, crawled or sat up. She could not even turn over, and was completely helpless. The only response we ever got from Connie was an occasional smile, while Carol, her younger sister, could get a giggle at times. The doctor was amazed at Connie's condition every time Mary took her for a visit. He always had words of praise for the way she nursed and took care of her.

Nine years after Connie was born in May of 1955, our little daughter Carol was born healthy. Mary mothered and cared for both Connie and Carol for four more years when in July of 1959 our son Bill was born. We knew at this point with two more young children that it was time for us to make a decision about Connie's care. We prayed a lot, and talked with our Doctor, our friends and relatives.   The Doctor agreed with our decision to place Connie into a care facility and told us there was a hospital in Porterville that was highly recommended for individuals in her condition. When Bill was three months old, and with tears in our eyes, we registered Connie in the hospital.

Just four weeks after placing Connie in the care facility, we were visiting my folks at Belridge. In the middle of the night we received a phone call that our little Connie had passed away. After the shock passed, Mary said, "We need to pray". We both knelt beside the bed and I MOVED MY POWERLINE A LITTLE TO THE RIGHT, to the Cross of Jesus Christ. Together we committed our lives to Him, and promised that our children would be raised in a Christian home, that we would love God first, and then love others with His love. Over the years, we have done our best to keep that promise; to know our children is to know that it was true.

Later, when our children were older, Mary thought she would like to get a job. We all thought she should do it, and agreed to help her with the chores around the house. Mary got a job as a teacher's assistant at a school for the handicapped working with children like Connie. She worked there thirteen years. Today she says, "It was a job I loved, and even got paid for it." Isn't my Mary the greatest!!

IT WAS A TOUGH DANCE BABE BUT TOGETHER WE MADE IT.

This chapter eight, because of my great love for Connie, was most difficult for me to write. It's hard to see with tears in my eyes most of the time. It was really hard when I lost a good portion of it in my computer. I was ready to throw in the towel on the whole thing. So let me do something easy in closing this chapter.

I want to share an e-mail I received the other day.

"Having four visiting family members coming, my wife was very busy, so I offered to go to the store for her to get some needed items, which included light bulbs, paper towels, trash bags, detergents and Clorox. So off I went. I scurried around the store, gathered up my goodies and headed for the checkout counter, only to be blocked in a narrow aisle by a young man who appeared to be about sixteen-years-old. I wasn't in a hurry, so I patiently waited for the boy to realize that I was there. This was when his hands went excitedly in the air and declared in a loud voice, "Mommy, I'm over here."

It was obvious now, he was mentally challenged and also startled as he turned and saw me standing so close to him, waiting to squeeze by. His eyes widened and surprise exploded on his face. I said, "Hey Buddy what's your name?" "My name is Denny and I'm shopping with my mother," he responded proudly. "Wow," I said "That's a cool name; I wish my name was Denny, but my name is Steve." "Steve, like Stevarino?" he asked, "yes" I answered. "How old are you, Denny?" "How old am I now, mommy?" he asked his mother as she slowly came over from the next aisle. "You're fifteen-years-old Denny; now be a good boy and let the man pass-by."

I acknowledged her and continued to talk to Denny for

several more minutes about summer, bicycles and school. I watched his brown eyes dance with excitement, because he was the center of someone's attention. He then abruptly turned and headed toward the toy section. Denny's mom had a puzzled look on her face and thanked me for taking the time to talk with her son. She told me that most people wouldn't even look at him, much less talk to him. I told her that it was my pleasure and then I said something I have no idea where it came from, other than by prompting of the Holy Spirit. I told her that there are plenty of Red, Yellow, and Pink Roses in God's Garden; however, "Blue Roses" are very rare and should be appreciated for their beauty and distinctiveness.

You see, Denny is a "Blue Rose" and if someone doesn't stop and smell that rose with their heart and touch that rose with their kindness, then they've missed a blessing from God. She was silent for a second and then with a tear in her eye she asked, "Who are you?" Without thinking I said, "Oh I'm probably just a Dandelion, but I sure love living in God's garden." She reached out, and squeezed my hand and said, "God bless you!" and then I had tears in my eyes."

May I suggest the next time you see a BLUE ROSE, don't turn your head and walk off. Take time to smile and say Hello. Why? Because, by the grace of God, this mother or father could be you.

For many years after our little Connie was born, I remembered my talk with my Navy buddy, Henry. I lived in a state of hell over it. Could the three years of setting over those radar machines been responsible for Connie's condition? Am I the reason for her broken little body? At times I hated myself, I hated the Navy and I hated life itself. How cruel of me to know of a problem I might have had, and secretly pass it on to my little girl. I never told or talked with anyone about it; I just lived with it. At one point, I thought I could drink it from my mind. But one night, sick from booze, with Connie on my lap and Mary driving, I decided that was not the way to handle things.

War had been hell: it had destroyed my goals and dreams, it destroyed my scholarship, it destroyed a sport that I dearly loved, it destroyed a career that I dreamed of, it had taken three years of my life that I would never get back, and because of the war my precious little daughter lived in a broken body; but I would be damned if I would allow it to destroy my marriage.

I decided to live with it.

Over time we talked with different doctors that explained Connie's condition was due to birth trauma. Eventually, Mary began to talk about wanting another child, but I was still secretly afraid that my years as a radar man might effect another child. I came up with all kinds of excuses as I kept putting Mary off while not wanting to discuss another baby. Finally, when Connie was eight years old and I was still a little fearful, we decided to have another child. After a year of daily pleading to God, He delivered Carol to us and four years later Bill. Both babies were in good health. I didn't have that fear anymore thanks be to God.

James William Huckaby
"Mr. Huck"

Connie's Final Resting Place

My theology has not explained to me who gets Blue Roses, but I will say this: we loved and adored every little bone in Connie's frail little body. We tried to make her as comfortable as possible. She was the most precious thing in our lives, and it took just one of her little smiles to break our hearts. Be patient Connie, winter is almost over, and we are looking forward to seeing you.

James William Huckaby
"Mr. Huck"

Chapter Nine

MY PRINCESS

*"You have one childhood with your daughter;
when it's gone, it's gone for eternity.
I feel like I've been handed a prize orchid,
And I can't grow a weed."
- Richard Paul Evans*

Our Carol

It's mid-summer of 1954, and we are spending the summer at our camp at Huntington Lake. For several years we had set up a nice camp in June, well above the lakefront campgrounds, and Mom, Mary, and Connie would stay there for most of the summer. Dad and I would go up on weekends, and during our vacation time.

One year the Park Ranger stopped by and told us that in the future we could only stay in the camp grounds for two weeks at a time, and no longer stay the entire summer. After eating lunch that day my father disappeared all afternoon. When he came back he said, "I JUST BOUGHT A CABIN." We all climbed into the car to go see his purchase. When we got there it was just a broken down shack. It was a total wreck, and I said, "Dad what do you expect to do with this junk pile?" "We will tear it all down, clean it up, and build a new cabin", he said. *"*Dad" I said, "I've only ever built a chicken coop, and you've only built a dog house, and you want to build a cabin at 7,000 foot elevation that is snowed in all winter?"

"Bud," he said, "we can do it."

In the spring of 1955, Belridge Oil Company sold my father a small building that he tore down for the lumber. On Friday, May 22, 1955, he loaded it in a borrowed truck and trailer, and drove it up to the cabin site where I met him later that night. We decided that there was too much snow to do anything, but would unload the truck and trailer in the morning, and start building two weeks later. Next morning I was sleeping away in my sleeping bag when I felt a nudge on my head. I awoke to see a strange man standing there. He said, "Are you Mr. Huckaby?" I replied, "Yes". He said, "YOU GOT A NEW

BABY GIRL". My PRINCESS had arrived two weeks early! I had heard or read somewhere that there was a special bond between a father and his daughter; and as I looked at that precious healthy little bundle for the first time, I knew that the saying would be true for a life time.

Three weeks later, Carol would make her first visit up to the cabin site. We contacted the doctor to see if it would be all right to take her at this age, and he said to just keep her nice and warm and she would be just fine. The weekend before, Dad and I had built two nice tent houses. We had hooked them up with electricity, and had a flush toilet in a small building close by. We were all set for the princess, and she did fine.

It took five years to build the cabin as we had only the summer months to work on it. There was too much snow during the winter to even get to the cabin. Every weekend, every holiday, and every vacation day would find my father and mother, and the four of us at the cabin site. On our lot was a 14' x 14' building that was in good condition. We moved in an old wood cook stove, a table, and five chairs, and it became our chow hall. My mother took over the old stove and turned out some great meals, plus great pies and cakes. I tell you all this just to say that when Carol was a little over three years old, my father promised Carol that when the cabin was completed, she could have the old chow hall. I would tear it all down, and build her a play house from the lumber. True to his word, when the cabin was livable, the chow hall building was Carol's.

Carol got her playhouse

I tore the old building down and built Carol's play house in the drive way just in front of the cabin's garage. I built it just like the cabin with high pitched roof, board and batt siding, gingerbread molding around the door and two windows. It turned out real cute, and dad was real excited to see it when he drove up the drive way. I put it together using bolts so we unbolted it, laid each side on top of the trailer, and I took it to Fresno to set it up in the back yard. I built a little table and two little benches to fit inside. On Sunday after lunch you would find Carol, Mary, and Sue (Carol's dear little friends), setting in the playhouse going over what Carol had learned in Sunday School that day.

I know that everyone, friend or relative, has heard the Bull Dog story; but it was the first display of Carols' "never give up on a challenge" attitude. Dorothy and Bill Eckart lived across the street from us, and Bill and I worked for the same company. One day Mom took our baby Billy over to show him off to Dorothy, when Carol discovered that Dorothy had just gotten a little Boston

Terrier puppy. Dorothy 'ooohd and ahhhed' over Billy, while Carol 'ooohd and ahhhed' over the puppy. Dorothy said to Carol, "How about we trade you the puppy for Billy?" "Sure!" said Carol. Four year old Carol marched back across the street and said, "Daddy, where are Billy's clothes kept?" "In the bedroom," I said "why?" Carol said, "I just traded him for a puppy and I need all of his clothes." How do you convince a crying little girl that she is to young for a puppy and maybe in a few years she could have a dog and still keep her little brother?

All the neighborhood kids learned to swim in a two foot deep pool at the elementary school next door. They had two lifeguards to teach, and watch over them as they all played. Let's see, there were Mary, Carol, Sue, Monie, and Leanne. I know that there were more, but that was the group that are like sisters today. Sometimes the girls would all come over to the house for a sleep-over. What a sight to see them in their sleeping bags all over the den floor, and Billy standing at the door looking sad because he was a boy and had to stay out. After elementary school, they all moved from Dailey Grammar School down the street about five blocks to go to Hamilton middle school. Three years later they would go two more blocks south to Fresno high school. Mary was a year older than Carol, and Sue was a year younger, so she had one of those girls with her all through school. During their teen years, the girls were active in the youth group at church during the week, and church camp in the summer; they were all getting good Christian teaching.

There was a young man named Pat Hurley who was a youth evangelist working for Campus Crusade for Christ.

He would pass through town during their high school years, and all the kids loved him. During Carol's first year of college, news got out that Pat was in town and there would be a very important meeting at Bretzs' house at 6:00pm that night. Carol got the word and she was anxious to see what Pat was up to. By 1:30am in the morning, Carol was not home yet and I was upset and concerned. So I got up, got dressed, and drove to the Bretz's house.

Carol's little VW bug was setting in the drive-way so I knew that she was all right, so I turned around and drove back home. All I could think of was how I was going to give Pat a lecture about keeping kids out that late. Carol returned home soon after I got home, and I didn't see her until dinner the next night. She sat down at the table and announced, "I went to the Bullard High School today and got permission to start a bible study there. A Mormon teacher has allowed me to use his room, and it starts next Tuesday. That was what the meeting was all about last night." I never ever talked to Pat or even my princess about what I had done. Years later at two different churches, I met two young ladies, both married with children, who ask me if I knew Carol and I said "yes". They then told me they were in her bible study class at Bullard High School and how much her teaching had meant to them in their later years.

As best as I can remember, during Carol's junior year at Fresno Pacific College, a new young man showed up at our house. What was sort of amusing is that he was always lying in the hallway, directly under the old swamp cooler, just panting away; much as a puppy might do. I thought, laughing to myself, maybe Carol had at last gotten her puppy. The boys' name was Tim, and he was from Oregon; which explained why he couldn't stand Fresno's 100+ degree temperatures during the summer. Tim was a very nice looking Christian boy - just the kind of lad any dad would like to have as a son-in-law. However, if this relationship developed, I knew that Tim would steal my Princess away, and take her to Oregon. Later that year Tim was asking me if he could take Carol to Oregon to meet his parents. I could see myself losing ground because I envisioned them coming back to Fresno engaged to be married. SURE enough it happened: Carol came back with a sparkler on her left hand. Hardly seemed fair: Tim taking her 750 miles north so I could not be an influence.

Tim and Carol were married that summer, and finished their last year of college as husband and wife. They rented an apartment near the college, and they were close enough that we could see them often. It was easy to take them out to dinner or have a quick ice cream cone. Shortly after graduation, we were loading them up to move to Oregon. Bill had an old Ford van loaded to the hilt with a mattress tied on top. Tim and Carol had their VW bug loaded with a chest of drawers tied on top, and Mary and I followed with our Chrysler Cordoba. We looked like the "Okies" did back when they "took" California in 1935. The only difference was we were going to overtake Oregon. We arrived at Tim's parents house (Pete and Rubina), and in just two days we all got the kids moved into a one bedroom apartment in West Salem. Time passed quickly as it usually does, so it was time for hugs, kisses, and good-byes. I got in the car and started it, and when I looked up there in front of the car stood Tim, Carol, Rubina and Pete. "I can't do this!" I thought, "I can't leave my Princess. I'll go grab her and put her in the car", but my Princess had become Tim's wife, and now I had to share. With tears in my eyes I drove away.

Well, I went home and licked my wounds, and decided I just might be able to handle my daughter being in Oregon 700 miles away. Who was I going to say "HI PRINCESS" to now? I had to get my mind on other things. The kids were living in a one bedroom apartment so no room for us to stay with them, and I knew we should not impose on Pete and Rubina. So what do I do?

Then it came to me to get a travel trailer and take it to Oregon where I could set it up in a campground for the summer, and put it on a storage lot for the winter. The next summer we headed for Salem with a 26 foot travel trailer on the back of the old Cordoba for a two week vacation. This system worked very well for several years, but after we retired we bought a small mobile home in Salem.

Things went very well with Tim and Carol, and in two or three years they were in their own home in a nice neighborhood in Salem. Soon afterward, Carol was pregnant with their first child. The first thing on my mind was to find out if the bond between father and daughter was also true between granddaughter and grandfather. In a few months, little Tommy, our first grandchild was born. A few years later out popped Teddy, followed by Toby a few years after that. By this time, Cathy (our son Bill's wife), had also popped two boys and later she had two more. That made seven grandsons and no granddaughters - that is no way to treat a grandfather; BUT I love all my grandsons dearly. Tim and Carol have done very well over the years; they both have very good jobs, a beautiful home, and they're active in their church. Carol has been a Sunday school teacher for years. They are now empty nesters as their boys are no longer boys, they are grown men. At this time Tommy, his wife Jessica, and Toby live Bend, OR. While Teddy, his wife Julie, and daughters Holly and Anabel, live in Eugene, OR.

I received a Father's Day card yesterday from Carol. It was signed "Many, Many Memories! Thank you for them All. The P." You know what "The P" means? It means 'The Princess'. IS THE BOND STILL THERE? I say "yes yes yes!". I thank my God every day for a wonderful daughter like Carol.

Chapter Ten

MY PAL – MY FRIEND – MY SON

*"I have come to believe that the only true way to serve
God Is to serve His children."
- Richard Paul Evans*

Our Bill (William)

Are you trading diamonds for stones?

The foothills northwest of the little town of Coalinga, California are covered with asbestos mines. The asbestos is just exposed on the ground and can be scooped up with your hands. A manufacturing firm built a big plant to process and bag up the asbestos so they could use it in construction projects. The plant required an enormous amount of electricity, so to run service lines to them was quite a project. We had to run several miles of 70,000 volt transmission line to a substation, and then several more miles of 12,000 volt distribution line to the facility. Normally the transmission portion and the substation would have been handled by the San Francisco survey crews, but everything except the substation was assigned to us. On Monday I took two survey crews to the project: I worked with one crew on the 70,000 volt line and put the other crew on the 12,000 volt line. The whole project lasted five weeks, and we would stay in the town of Coalinga Monday through Friday.

Now I tell you all this to get to the point I want to make: one Friday when I got home, Billy came running up to me and said, "Daddy I learned to ride my bicycle while you were gone," and he hopped on his bike and rode to the corner and back. One of a small boy's greatest accomplishments is riding his bike for the first time without training wheels; and I missed it. I was gone away from home and had traded a diamond for a stone.

A few years down the road we let Billy have a paper route. He delivered the daily papers after school on his own, but on Sundays I would help him with those big fat papers loaded with advertisements. We had to deliver the paper early in the morning before church, so he and I would load the papers in the back of the car; I would fold them and give them to Billy and he would toss them to the house. Every Sunday after we finished our route we headed for Winchell's Doughnut House and had hot chocolate (coffee) and doughnuts. What a great treat, and we were really BONDING - an entire hand full of diamonds instead of stones.

Billy was born on July 6 1959. About 3:00pm I took Mary to the hospital. When we got there the nurse told me to go take a seat in the waiting room and she would call me back in when they had Mary settled. I waited, and I waited, and I waited. I knew good and well that Mary told the nurse to leave me out there because I would drive her crazy if she didn't. The next thing I heard was, "Mr Huckaby, you have a son." Finally I got to go give both Mary and my new son big kisses. The nurse told me that the doctor said at the birthing, "My God look at those shoulders, we have another football player." My memories of that late night talk I had with my friend Henry, a fellow radar man during the war, was never far from my mind at times like this. I Thanked God for another healthy child.

Bill grew fast as he learned that:

> 1) Kenny (the neighborhood bully) a boy two years older would take away his toys and hit him to make him cry, and then tickle him to make him laugh before Mary could get there.

> 2) That when the girls were in the playhouse playing with their Troll Dolls, it was off limits for him

3) That his world was full of girls, and no boys for friends. He and Carol could play together, but when a couple of girls showed up - he was poison.

He soon learned that the playground next door was the place for fun, and he found there a playground director named Jackie that loved him. She showed him how to do crafts, and help them make floats for the kid's parade downtown. The lifeguards taught him to swim, and he got to make friends with the GUYS.

When Bill was in about the second or third grade, he made a friend that lived just north of the playground that required crossing a busy street in Fresno called Shields. I had cautioned him that he was not to cross Shields unless one of us was with him. Well, oops it happened one day, when I got home from work Bill was gone and I found him across Shields at his friend's house. When we got home I told him to go wait in the den, and think of why he had disobeyed us. We had a ping pong table set up in the den, so when I came in the den I grab a ping pong paddle and told him to bend over. I swatted him on his fat little butt about six times. Now think for a minute: a ping pong paddle about one quarter of an inch thick on heavy Levi Jeans, and lord knows what he had in his pockets, that's got to smart a little bit – NOT! That was the first time, and the last time I ever paddled Bill.

Bill followed Carol through the same schools only he was four years behind. He was a good student, lettered in football and track in high school, and was active in the church youth group. The fellowship hall at the church was set up with a basketball court inside. After the church was locked up each night, Bill and his good friend

John had a secret way of breaking into the fellowship hall. The two of them would get in and shoot some hoops all by themselves. One night they got a little wild and broke a window. They had to go to Pastor Dick and explain how they got in, what they were doing, and why. Pastor Dick, being the good guy that he was, worked out a deal with the boys and nobody else knew what happened.

I think that it was early in the summer after Bill's sophomore year in high school that I decided to go home for lunch one day. I heard a noise in Bill's bedroom. I looked in and there was Bill and his buddy John flopped out on the bed. I said, "What's going on you all?" "Oh were just hanging out; nothing to do around here." they replied. "I'll help you guys out a little," I said, "get off your butts and get out and find a job, and see if that will relieve some of your pain O. K.." When I got home that night, I found out that they both got jobs working for a firm cleaning a car dealership's auto repair area. After High school Bill went to Fresno Pacific College (where Carol had gone) for one year. While he was there he got on with American Ambulance as an Emergency Medical Technician. Some time later American Ambulance sent Bill to Delta College in Stockton where he got his Paramedic Certificate.

It was about this time that Bill met Cathy; she worked as a nurse in the Emergency Room where he would transport patients. I'm sure she was the first person Bill looked for when they brought in a patient. My dear sweet Cathy - she melted my heart the first time I met her. Cathy was a Catholic convert and she was definitely turned on for Jesus Christ. That made her number one in my book. I encouraged Bill to keep her because she looked like a girl that could bring me a granddaughter to love and spoil. Well as we all know now, Carol would pop out three boys, and Cathy in turn popped out four more boys - me with no granddaughters and seven grandsons! I love my grandsons dearly and I admire each one for being the men they are today. Teddy and his wife finally brought two wonderful great-granddaughters, but they lived in Oregon and it's hard for me to spoil them from such a long distance. Bill decided to take a couple of years at Fresno City College and worked toward his Registered Nursing License; now he could work in the hospitals. Bill and Cathy were married in 1981 and it was time to move on.

Bill and Cathy moved from Fresno to Reno, Nevada where they both worked as nurses at the local hospital, and settled into a very nice new home. Mary and I enjoyed our visits with the kids, especially during Christmas. Christmas in Reno was quite a change from one in Fresno. Tim and Carol came with little Tommy that year and Bill, Tim, and I, spent several days on cold golf courses before we left for home.

Bill had the most beautiful Siberian Husky that I had ever seen; his name was Mishka and when he got loose, he was a runner. He got out one night and got hit by a car. Bill found him on the side of the road, had to have him put down. It tore Bill's heart out when he called me about it and it tore my heart out for Bill, knowing how much he loved Mishka. All I could do was to say, "Son, lets pray about it".

It was here in Reno where our first Huckaby grandson Josh was born - a good healthy boy. Things were good with their family now started, and their network of friends they had through the church they were active in. During this time Bill and Cathy entered into a "Wellness" business venture with a couple of doctors, nurse, and two respiratory therapists. It was a good business, but I think it was a little ahead of its time, and probably in the wrong city. The people of Reno were not quite ready for something like that, and the business failed.

Bill and Cathy ended up with a very big debt. They sold everything in Reno and (Bill, Cathy, and Josh) moved back to Fresno. Determined to pay off their debt, they worked two years, day and night (literally), at hospitals in Madera, Selma, and Fresno. Mary and I were thrilled to have them stay with us during this period because they were working so hard to make their final payment. Besides, we got to love our grandbaby Josh, and watched him grow for two years.

ONLY GOD CAN KNOW HOW PROUD I WAS OF HOW THE KIDS HANDLED THEIR OBLIGATION.

When their debt had been paid-in-full, they decided they needed a break so they took a couple of weeks and traveled around the north-west and decided on making their new home in Bend Oregon. Bend is a beautiful city right in the center of the State of Oregon. To the West you can see a forest of beautiful trees and The Sisters Mountains with all the winter activities. To the East you see the High Desert with miles and miles of open land.

The kids found a nice home in Bend, both found work at the hospital, and it was here their second son Luke was born. In all their moves, the first thing they do is to find a good church that they can get involved in. Not just a place for Sunday morning, but a place they can actively share the Love of God. For this I have been eternally proud of them.

During all of Bill's time in the hospital, he met a Perfusionist (one who operates the heart-lung machine in open heart surgery). After talking with him, and observing a case, Bill thought that was something he could do. He searched all of the Perfusion schools he could find (none of which were local), and applied to every one he was qualified for. One of those was in Wichita, Kansas that had a one year program. He went out and interviewed, and was notified later he had been accepted. They rented out their house in Bend, grabbed up the two boys and headed for Kansas.

One long year!!

Bill had been cautioned that he would not have time to work during school, so he could keep his nose in his books. Cathy would spend her time bringing home the bacon, beans and soup. The boys were busy being entertained by a wonderful little grandmother type baby-sitter who loved them very much. The year was over, Bill was a Perfusionist, Cathy is worn to a frazzle, the baby-sitter says she can't move with them, so in their old beat up hail-stoned dented Toyota they headed for California. Our two little grandbabies are now grown men and both have graduated from college. Josh is a Youth Director at a church in Madera, while Luke is on his way to post graduate study.

You all know the rest of the story. They settled in Lodi, California, and live in a beautiful home; where they have two more sons (our sixth and seventh grandsons): Ben who just finished his first year of college, and Jake starting his Junior year of high school. I think they say it all happened by the grace of God and hard work. I would say that I thank God every day for all of them.

I started this story with the quote, "Are you trading diamonds for stones?" The bonding that Bill and I have had is a relationship that I have cherished all my life. And there have been times when the diamonds have been huge. One was when we were just the two of us riding in a golf cart across the golf course. There were many and I wish there could have been more, but I got to old to swing a club. Another way I think is a good way to bond with your son is to build something. My father and I spent 5 years building a cabin at 7,000 foot elevation. My father is long gone, but the memories are still with me today. Bill and I built a two story fort for his boys in their back yard. It is probably a pink elephant in some ones yard now, but the memories of us building that fort are still with me today. BONDING - THAT'S THE THING TODAY.

The Fort

Hi Babe, another dance has come and gone by the way side, and it was great while it lasted. The kids are long gone but the memories are still there. I think that one of the memories we have left for them to remember about us is the vow that we made before God on our wedding day. Keep it holy, keep it strong. Please join me my sweet; I think it's time for another dance.

James William Huckaby
"Mr. Huck"

I love this e-mail which I received the other day:

What Is A Boy?

Between the innocence of baby food and the dignity of manhood we find a delightful creature called a boy. Boys come in assorted sizes, weights, and colors, but all boys have the same creed. To enjoy every second of every minute of every hour of every day and to protest with noise, their only weapon, when their last minute is finished and the adult males pack them off to bed at night.

Boys are found everywhere --- on top of, underneath, inside of, climbing on, swinging from, running around or jumping to. Mothers love them, little girls hate them, older sisters and brothers tolerate them, adults ignore them, and Heaven protects them. A boy is truth with dirt on his face, beauty with a cut on his finger, wisdom with bubble gum in his hair, and the hope of the future with a frog in his pocket.

When you are busy, a boy is inconsiderate, bothersome, an intruding jangle of noise. When you want him to make a good impression, his brain turns to jelly, or he becomes a savage, sadistic jungle creature bent on destroying the world and himself with it.

A boy is a composite --- he has the appetite of a horse, the disposition of a sword swallower, the energy of a pocket-size atomic bomb, the curiosity of a cat, the lungs of a dictator, the imagination of a Paul Bunyan, the shyness of a violet, the audacity of a steel trap, the enthusiasm of a fire cracker, and when he makes something he has five thumbs on each hand.

He likes ice cream, knives, saws, Christmas, comic books, the boy across the street, the woods, water, in its natural habitat, large animals, Dad, Saturday mornings, trains and fire engines. He is not much for Sunday School, company, schools, books without pictures, music lessons, neckties, barbers, girls, overcoats, adults or bedtime.

Nobody else is so early to rise, or so late to supper. Nobody else gets so much fun out of trees, dogs, and Frisbees. Nobody else can cram into one pocket a rusty knife, a half eaten apple, three feet of string, an empty Bull Durham sack, two gum drops, six cents, a sling-shot, a chunk of unknown substance, and a genuine supersonic code ring with a secret compartment.

A boy is a magical creature---- you can lock him out of your work shop, but you can't lock him out of your heart. You can get him out of your study, but you can't get him out of your mind. Might as well give up----- he is your captor, your jailor, your boss, and your master-----a freckled- face, pint size, cat chasing, bundle of noise. But, when you come home at night with only the shattered pieces of your hopes and dreams, he can mend them like new with the two magic words: "Hi Dad."

My Bill

Chapter Eleven

MY TWO LITTLE PIXIES

*"Don't put your spoon in another man's soup.
There is nothing so healing as to heal another."
- Richard Paul Evans*

My Pixies with Carol

Do blessings come in twos? I think so because there were two that blessed our home when we moved in on Farris Avenue in Fresno; and they have continued to bless us until this day. The blessings come in the form of two darling little girls that lived across the alley from us: Mary (one year older than Carol), and Sue (one year younger than Carol). The sisterly bond that grew between these three little girls will last forever. Why, you ask? Because they love each other with the love of Jesus Christ. All three are happily married and have raised their children in Christian homes. A delight to all who know them; if any doubt, go ask the guy that adopted them decades ago.

It's June 2, 1957, Mary and I have signed the papers that will let us move into our new house the following Saturday. I have about half of the things in the house when I hear a tap tap tap on the door. There stands two little girls, the older one says, "Can Carol play?" My God I haven't got moved in yet and kids are here to play. "What is your name?" I ask. "I'm Mary" replies the oldest, "I'm three years old and we live just around the corner." I look at the little one and she timidly just says "Sue" and nothing more. I call for my Mary for help, and she answers, "Carol met them at the playground yesterday, they are harmless bring them in." Just two more kids I had to step over while I'm trying to get the sofa in the house. God seemed to say, "Get used to it, for the next sixty years this house will be filled with kids you will have to step around." Finally the girls went outside. I watched them as they marched down the walk. Mary (3), Carol (2), and Sue (1), were like a group of little ducklings.

Carol was never without at least one of these little girls with her. When Carol was in kindergarten, Mary was in the first grade. When Carol was in the first grade, all three of the girls were together through grade school. Mary graduated first but Sue was still with Carol. When Carol graduated and went to middle school, Mary was right there to welcome her. When Mary graduated middle school, Sue was there with Carol for her last year. That was the same all through high school.

In high school, all three girls were excellent swimmers, and they joined the synchronized swimming team. They were also the letter girls, flag wavers, and into all the activities that made color for the football games. College took them in different directions, but their friendship never suffered. Since Mary was the oldest she was the first to go to college. She was an Agriculture Major, so right at dinner time she'd come into the house with an exciting story to tell us right out of the cow barn while we ate. Some of them would have been better told at another time and place, but for Mary they were to exciting to keep. We loved Mary so we also loved her stories.

When Mary and Sue were about ages 8 and 10, their father passed away and I felt so sorry for them. So young to be without a father; it broke my heart knowing how important it was to have a father in the family. I spent a lot of time in prayer about how I could help. God seemed to tell me to show them a lot of love. Don't try to take their fathers place, but be there for them if they needed someone. Over the years I begin to feel that father-daughter bond (which I wrote about in chapter nine) develop between me and my two little girls. I grew to love them with the same love I shared with Carol; these two pixies had a place in my heart for sure.

Well time goes by as time always does, and girls will grow into young women, and start thinking about young boys as girls do. Mary had a thing going on with a young man named Will. Now Will was a good old boy whom we had known almost as long as Mary had. He lived just around the block from us, and had gone to the same

schools as the girls. He also had been active in the
youth group at different church. All in all, we were
excited when Mary popped the news that she and Will
were going to get married. They had a beautiful
wedding, a wonderful life together, raised two beautiful
daughters, and now live in Madera, California.

I spent all of chapter nine telling you about how Tim
came in and stole Carol right out from under my nose,
and then ran off with her taking her all the way to Salem,
Oregon. They were married at the same church as Will
and Mary. Shortly after Carol's wedding, Sue
occasionally mentioned a new name to us: a boy named
Randy. Now Randy was not one of the youth group or
one of the neighborhood guys. Turns out Sue met him
at state college; and was a stranger to all of us.

Who was this fellow dating our Sue? Seems that our
Sue had an invitation from Randy's parents to come up
and visit with them in Ripon for a Sunday afternoon
dinner. We were totally impressed with Randy and his
parents - a wonderful Christian Family. Any doubts
about Randy were erased forever. The way he looked
into Sue's eyes had to be real love. A short time later,
they were married in the same church as the other two
girls. Randy and Sue eventually moved to Wenatchee,
Washington, and also raised their family of two boys and
one girl in a fine Christian home. The two pixies gave
me the greatest honor of my life when both of them
asked me to give them away at their wedding. THANKS
GIRLS.

I would hope and pray that during my efforts to be
involved in the lives of these little girls, that I have never
offended or embarrassed or discouraged them. If I have,

I am so sorry, and I hope they will forgive me. My intentions were only to help heal the loss of their father.

Before I move on with this story, there is one thing more I must share. It seemed that almost every night during the week there was a bible study going on in our house. One night while the study was moving along there was a knock at the door; a strange young man was there. He introduced himself and said that he was just passing through town. He had called our pastor to find out if anything was going on, was told about the bible study, and said, "So here I am." We welcomed him in, and he joined all the others.

On another night there was another knock on the door – this time it was Helen. Helen was Mary and Sue's mother. Before the night was over, Helen said a sinner's prayer and gave her life to Jesus Christ. She said she wanted what her girls had.

When my children were young, around ages 10 and 6, my company decided I should spend the summer in our San Francisco office learning their land department procedures. I would fly up on Monday morning, and fly back Friday afternoon. Three months away from my family. The kids thought this was a treat because after the plane took off they had hot chocolate and cinnamon toast before they left the airport. On Friday afternoon they met me as I was coming off the plane (in those days you could walk right out to the plane, no TSA) with lots of hugs and kisses for me.

During my three months there, I would spend one month in their mapping and plotting section, another month in their surveying section, and the third month in their document writing section. The month I spent in the surveying section found me the first week with a full survey crew out in the field. The second week I spent running one of their crews, and the third and fourth week I spent with two different field engineers.

Now a field engineer was the next step above a surveyor. They supervised the surveyors, and searched records in the court house. The job required a license by the state of California, and it paid a nice amount of money. I admired these men, and thought the job would be an interesting challenge.

It was the last day of my 90 day sentence, and had served my time with good conduct. I was saying goodbye to some friends I had made, when in walked Al; the senior field engineer from the surveying section. He asked me, "Could I come down to Jack's office, he wanted to talk to me before I left." Jack was in charge of the entire San Francisco surveying department. He asked how I had enjoyed my time in San Francisco, and he thanked me for coming. He said that he was going to fire one of his surveyors, and told me if I would be willing to take his position, he would put me on the list for the next opening for a field engineer.

Now here was the job of a life time for me: one that I had dreamed about and spent years preparing for. All the studying I did to prepare to pass the state license test, and all of the experience I gained from the different jobs I had worked had prepared me to handle a job as a Field Engineer. I knew several of them, and had done work for them in the past. The one that I expected I might replace was an engineer who was occasionally used as an "Expert Witness" in court cases. I had suspected that

Jack might offer something like this, so it was not a total surprise, and I had been in a lot of prayer about it. The main plus was the big increase in pay, and my family could use the extra money. The big negative was that Jack's work would take me all over the state. I would be gone almost every week, and only home on the weekends. It seemed that God was asking, "Which was most important to me: the big bucks, or my family." It took me all of about five minutes to say, "Thanks, but no thanks." to my friend Jack, and that I wanted to go back to Fresno. I was proud to say my kids came first. However, I did find out when I got home, they had given me a title change with a few extra bucks. I was no longer a senior surveyor, but a Principal Surveyor; the only one in the entire P.G.&E system.

At this point I took over the entire surveying section in Fresno, and had the authority to assist surveyors throughout the San Joaquin Division. I was out-of-town occasionally, but was able to spend a great deal of time with my family. God seemed to say family first takes the place of big bucks real fast when you love your kids. Remember that during this time I had two more little girls I was trying to show my love to.

Funny, or Too Much Wine

Over the years the girls, all of my friends and relatives that lived in Fresno called me "Mr Huck", as they still do to this day. Because I am so much older than most of the people here, the name "Mr Huck" to me has the same meaning as the "Hi Dad" of the email in the previous chapter.

It meant I love you.

Chapter Twelve

IN THE WORD

"God the source of all destiny, healing, and hope
I've read that the same breeze that extinguishes
some flames just fans others.
I still don't know what kind of flame I am."
- Richard Paul Evans

MY midlife crisis:

I guess if you ask my kids about it they would say
something like "Dad ain't cool no more. He needs some
time to find himself. Some time to lay back and let it all
hang loose, a week at church camp or a dip in those
spiritual springs". That's kind of where I was at this point
in my life. I had served in every position I had been ask
to do at the church: Chairman of the Board, Sunday
School Superintendent, and even tried to teach an adult
Sunday Class; it just wasn't there. I needed something.
WHATEVER COULD IT BE?

I'm sitting on a bench at the tennis court with my good
friend Bill Norby. Bill had just trounced me three straight
sets, and we were cooling off for the fourth; hopefully
this would be the one I could win. Bill was always
looking for something to do. Like the Sunday we were
talking in the front of our brand new church, he
interrupted the conversation with, "Jim lets paint the old
church." The old church had been changed into our
fellowship hall, and it looked a little ratty. Just like that,
Bill had it all set up with a few members for the next
Saturday, and away we went. It took a couple of

evenings to complete it but, it looked nice along side our new church building.

Another time I got a call from Bill saying that the loft where the organ pipes were to be installed had been painted black, and I mean black, and Bill said it had to be painted white. He said, "See you tomorrow night at 6:30." It took another night and a second coat of paint. A couple of days later, I received another call from Bill, "Jim, remember the loft we painted white? It has to be black again. See you tomorrow at 6:30." Bill was the first one to call when things needed to be done at the church, and I think I was the first on Bill's list to call when he needed help. Bill carried his golf clubs and his tennis racket in the back of his car. He was ready for either game at a moments notice.

Back to the bench at the tennis court, Bill said, "Jim did you know that Gerry, Charlie, and Max are all going to a nearby church for bible study? Let's go see what's going on over there." Gerry and Charlie were both good tennis players too, Bill and I had played them in doubles several times. I enjoyed playing Gerry because he was left handed. I had to change my game plan when I played him. His game seemed to be just the opposite of what I expected. Gerry's wife Lorena, was a saint; anyone with a problem would call on Lorena for prayer. There were times when she would ask me to talk to someone and, even though I was hesitant to do it, I would because I knew she would be praying for me.

Back at the bench again, I agreed with Bill that it wasn't fair for our friends to sneak off to a foreign church and go to a new bible study without us. So, the following Monday night we made a surprise visit to get all the dope. It was called Men's Bible Study Fellowship with about 150 to 200 men in attendance. There was also a Woman's Bible study Fellowship in Fresno, and both groups were spread throughout the State. It is a very in-depth study of the bible, and the study going on at that time was The Life and Letters of Paul. There were scriptures to read, questions and answers for each day of the week. One would allow at least one hour a day for study. Bill and I signed up for the next class and got our papers for the next week. When I got home, I went up stairs and changed my alarm from 6:00 to 5:00am, then went back down stairs and cleaned off my desk. I thought that I had found my, "WHATEVER COULD IT BE." Little did I realize that Bible Study Fellowship (BSF) would keep me busy for the next ten years.

When we arrived, we would start out in the sanctuary for an introduction to that evening's lesson. Then the group would split off into smaller groups and go to various classrooms on the church campus. The two hundred men were divided into groups of ten to twelve students, and each group had one person called a Discussion Leader who was in-charge of leading them through the question and answer period that lasted about an hour. After the Q & A session, we would return to the church sanctuary for a lecture by the leader of the program who at this time was a man named Ted. This repeated week after week until June when the city schools let out, and we would stop for the summer. I think the next years lesson was a study on the Gospel of St. Matthew. It started when the city schools started in September. About the middle of our second or third year, my dear friend Bill discovered that he had a brain tumor. In less than a year he passed away. I was totally destroyed as Bill had been one of my very best friends. I think that it was in his memory that I stuck with the program so long.

During the middle of my fourth year with BSF, our leader Ted approached me and asked if I would become a Discussion Leader. That was a real shock to me, and caught me totally off guard. I told Ted I would need some time to pray about it. He said, "Meet me at Denny's for coffee at 6:00am next Thursday." By this time I'd been in class with at least four different Discussion Leaders, and I admired each one of them. I had to ask myself could I do this. Conversation did not come easy for me, even today. I'm the kind of guy that will not say two words if one will do the job. Could I keep 10 men in discussion for a whole hour? I met with Ted at Denny's, and the first question he asked me was, "Did I have more than one wife" (meaning had I been divorced and remarried). If I had said yes, we would both have walked out of Denny's right then. One wife was a must. I explained to him what my problems were, but Ted still said to, "Give it a try". He said that he would use me as a sub when one of the other leaders could not be there. Discussion Leaders were required to meet two hours every Saturday morning to go over all the questions and be prepared for the following Monday night.

Ted finished his five year term when the classes ended that June, and a new leader took over the study. His name was Noel, and had been a Discussion Leader for years. He was a Civil Engineer whom I knew through the private company he worked for. He was also the brother-in-law of the teacher whom Mary worked with. That year Noel assigned me to lead the group of new men that would come each week to try our BSF. I started the first week with about 6 men. The second week I picked up three more men, but of the six men I had the first week, four had decided they didn't want to continue because they didn't have the time to devote to the study. It went that way all through the year as I don't think there was more than four or five men that stuck out the entire year. Noel always said, "Hang in there Jim, things will be different next year."

True to his word, he assigned me eleven men that stayed almost through the entire year: men from all walks of life, young and old, rich and poor. Another of my duties as a group leader was to call each man in the middle of the week to talk with them, and encourage them with their studies. I felt strange asking an eye surgeon, and an airline pilot if I could help with their lessons, but they were just like the rest of the guys: a little behind, but they would be caught up by Monday. I have a ton of stories I could tell from my ten years in BSF, but there are just three that I would like to share; two from this group, and one from the next year's group.

Herb was a few years older than I was, and he lived with his mother; he was probably her sole support. Every meeting I would ask for prayer requests, and each night Herb would ask for prayer for his mothers eyes as she had a difficult time reading. Each week he would share it was getting worse, and that he could not afford to take her to a doctor. We missed Herb for a couple of weeks, but when he did show up he came in praising God all over the place. He claimed that God had led him to Bible Study Fellowship, and then specifically to our group where he met an eye doctor. The doctor saw Herb's mother and saw that she got the care she needed, and so she could now read her Bible again. Herb knew that God alone was responsible for his mother's good vision, and he shared this testimony almost every time I asked for prayer requests. God loved Herb and so did I.

The second man named Ray was in his early 20's, and was a little on the nervous and anxious side. My habit during prayer time was that if I felt that a prayer request needed a little more attention, I would ask that person to remain after class and we would get a little more involved in his problem, and take more time for prayer. It was quite a little walk from our class room to the sanctuary, and this night there was no one to talk with so I left after the group left. Ray walked up to me and said, "Jim can I walk with you?" I replied, "Sure Ray." Then he said, "Jim, how can I be just like you?" "WHY?" I asked. "Well, look how you know the bible, how you can pray so easy, how nice you dress, you drive a nice car, all those things. Who would not want that." "Ray," I said, "we need to pray about that. Meet me in the chapel after the lecture."

Sure enough there he sat in the chapel chewing on his finger nails. "Ray, you hurt me because you are looking at the messenger and missing the message. I'm here to tell you that God loves you just like you are. He has plans for you, your job is to seek out what those plans are and fulfill them. Don't try to mold your life after man, but mold it after God. The clothes I wear are the same clothes I wore on Sunday, the car I drive is five years old and I got it used. These things mean nothing to me. Luke 12: 31 says, 'Seek his kingdom, and these things will be given to you as well.' I love you Ray, seek Him, because he has great things for you in your future. If you are looking at me, then I have failed because my job is to keep you looking at Jesus."

James William Huckaby
"Mr. Huck"

I had just sat down to one of my favorite dinners that Mary had prepared, round steak, and fried potatoes. My son Bill claims he was nineteen years old before he knew there were other cuts of meat besides round steak. There's a story there that I will tell later. Our kitchen was very small, and only had room for a small table that when the four of us got around it, there was very little room to spare.

After a bite or two the phone rang, and the way we are all squeezed in it took awhile to get on the line. "Hello", I said. "Hello Jim, this is Ray and my little girl ran away from home and I don't know what to do. Should I call the police or what?" I asked, "Ray how do you know she ran away?" "She said this morning that she was going to run away." he responded. "Ray, it's just 5:00 pm, maybe there is something going on at school. Wait a little bit before you call the cops. Meanwhile, let's take it to the Lord in prayer before you hang up. We had a short prayer, and I told him to hang in there a little while longer.

I finally got back to the table again and had a couple more bites when the phone rang again. "Hello", I said. "Jim, my little girl just walked into the house, and said she had been at a friend's house." "Wonderful Ray, I'm so glad for you. Let her know how much you love her, that you have made a great home for her, and to try to be happy there. And Ray, see if you can't get her interested in a good youth group at your church. See you next Monday night. Bye for now." As I returned to my dinner, all of my family had left the table, and my steak and fried spuds were cold. But God loved Ray and so did I.

I think it was the fourth year of my being a Discussion Leader. My new group was equally as nice as the previous group had been. There was a black man named Roy in this group, and I would guess he might have been a couple of years younger than me. He was very nice, but kind of quiet. He said very little during class, and did not enter much into the discussion about the lesson. Do not confuse him with Ray, Roy was black and Ray was white. Roy was at the meeting almost every Monday night. I learned from Roy that his wife was very sick, and was on dialysis since her kidneys were in very serious condition.

It was my habit to get to the meeting about fifteen minutes early and spend that time in the chapel for prayer. Roy got to the church during that time period, and could not find me. He asked one of the leaders where I might be. He told Roy I was in the chapel, and asked him if he wanted him to go get me. Roy said no, but to tell me that his wife had died, and he would not be at the meeting that night. Roy drove all the way across town to tell me why he would not be in class. That was how dedicated Roy was in his faith.

Now I tell you all this because I felt that I alone had to go to Roy's wife memorial service. Roy's wife was in charge of music ministries at her church. The service started with several beautiful numbers by the church choir. I quickly learned that there were churches from through out the valley at the service. Entire church choirs had attended, and except for one other individual, I was the only white person there. For the next three hours in a standing room only crowd, I listened to the most beautiful music I have ever experienced before or since. Thank you Roy for allowing me to be in your life for just a short while; I will always be in your debt.

Four and a half years as a student, five years as a Discussion Leader, and its time for me to move on to something else; but I enjoyed every minute of it. I have learned so much from the men I met: twelve new men every year eager to study the Word of God. Many of them far more knowledgeable about the Bible than I, but willing to share with the class where they were with their relationship with Christ. The two hours we Discussion Leaders spent together on Saturday mornings was a real treat. The one man who I remember most was the "Judge." Yes he was a true judge, it was interesting to hear stories how he dealt with the Word and the Court.

I leave you now with:

"It is a peculiar domain the mind enters when one is asleep.
Why it chooses one landscape over another or horror over joy is the most baffling of mysteries."
- Richard Paul Evans

Do you ever dream when you're asleep? I do almost every night. I have three "get-up" times: 2:00 and 4:00 and 6:00 am. The 2:00 and 4:00 are potty breaks; so that means I get in bed three times at night, which means I can have as many as three different dreams that night. I have never talked to a doctor about it for fear he will put me in an asylum some where. Let me tell you about a most recent one.

A BIT OF NAVY HUMOR

When my ship was in Seattle, Washington for overhaul, Mary and I discovered a new song called Paper Dolls. It was "our song", and when I was at sea it reminded me of Mary.

[NOW FROM THIS POINT ON WE ARE IN A DREAM]
One night Henry (my fellow crew member) and I were on watch together. I said, "Henry, sing Paper Dolls for me." as he had a beautiful singing voice. Henry was on the surface radar and had to sit on a stool so he could see the scope. I was on the aircraft radar, so I was just sitting in a chair with my back to Henry. He got in high gear on Paper Dolls, and was giving it all he had. I was getting a little homesick thinking of my Mary, when some one tapped me on the shoulder and said, "How about a dance sailor?" I looked up and it was Mary - 2000 miles from home. I jumped up and we started dancing. Dance after dance we continued. Until finally Henry said, "Can I cut in?" I said, "Sure!" to my friend. He hopped off the stool and they started dancing, and I started singing Paper Dolls. I'm going to buy a paper doll, a doll that nobody's gonna steal, a doll that I can call my own.
[END OF DREAM]

I woke up and looked at the clock. It was my 2:00 am bathroom number one get up time. I took care of things, climbed back in bed, gave Mary a little swat on the tush, in which she replied "WHAT?" I said, "I just wanted to know if you and Henry finished your dance?" She whispered, "SHUT UP AND GO BACK TO SLEEP." Well I turned over, pulled up the covers, and thought that's the last time I'll dream a dance with her.

Chapter Thirteen

THE GIFT

Sometimes people forget that faith precedes miracle.
They say give me fire and then I will cut some firewood.
In the end, love wins
- Richard Paul Evans

Uncle Walt & Aunt Alva with load of wrapped raisins

As I remember, I think that back in Chapter 12, I said the Men's Bible Study Fellowship group was studying the 'Life and Letters of Paul'. I don't recall where we started, but I do remember that Paul's First Letter to the Corinthian Church gave me a difficult time: chapters 12, 13, and 14 talk about Spiritual Gifts that edify the church. Chapter 12, verse 7 talks about the gifts of wisdom, knowledge, faith, healing, and miraculous powers. In verse 28 it says that in the church God has appointed apostles, prophets, teachers, workers of miracles, those having the gift of healing, those able to help others, gifts of administration or leadership, and those who speak in unknown languages. In Chapter 13, Paul speaks of the gifts of faith, hope, and love. Then Chapter 14 talks about the gifts of prophecy and tongues, and Paul instructs the Corinthian church in 12:31 to, "EAGERLY DESIRE THE GREATER GIFTS."

If I am going to serve the church as best as I can, I felt I needed to discover my special Spiritual Gift, and wondered how do I find out what it was? I prayed long and often about it, and one day God laid it out for me loud and clear. Let me lay the ground work for you.

My grandmother, on my mother's side, was a very dear to me. I learned a lot from her; she and grandpa lived on a farm, and all I remember was visiting them one day when I was about fours years old. Grandma says, "Let's take a walk." We walked out to the barn, and an old red rooster pecked her on her leg. She reached down and grabbed that old rooster by the head, swung her arm around about three times, the body of the rooster went flying across the barn, she threw the head down and said "that will teach him not to peck my leg." There was a big river that crossed the farm a short distance from the barn, and we walked down to watch the water flow. A cat had followed us from the barn to the river and brushed against grandmother's leg. She reached down, picked up the cat and said, "You need a bath" to the cat, and then threw the cat in the river. I learned a couple things that day. Don't touch Grandmothers leg, and be sure to take a bath every day.

James William Huckaby
"Mr. Huck"

GRANDMA
(This was my grandma Wilson when I was four years old; my mom gave this poem to me, but I'm sure my Grandmother had given it to her).

It read,

"I know what makes our grandma grand –
She always has a treat
A cookie or a piece of cake or apple pie to eat,
And when we go to visit her,
she gets the good things out,
And we don't have to ask for more
as long as she's about
Then ma will say,
"That's all today.
Don't give them any more.
You'll make them ill, I know you will
Tonight we'll walk the floor."
Our grandma never punishes or says that we are bad.
She always takes us on her knee and tells us she is glad
to have us racing around the house.
And when we get too smart
And Pa and Ma are awful cross,
she always takes our part
And once when I Had told a lie
And had to go to bed,
Without my tea, She came to me
And brought me jam and bread
Ma says it's funny Grandma acts
the way she does today
When she was Grandma's little girl, she couldn't disobey
Or only eat the things she liked and get a stomach-ache
Or pick the chocolate frosting off and never eat the cake.
When she was bad, she always had punishment to bear

> *But we can be much worse than she
> and Grandma doesn't care!"*

Grandma married a doctor named Macklewee
(something like that). He promised that he would teach
her how to be a nurse. Grandma said, "All he ever
taught [her] was how to have kids." Anyway, they had
three girls: Linda, Mary, and Alva. The doctor later died,
and on his death bed he asked his good friend James
William Wilson to take care of his family. I was named
James William after this grandpa.

Well James truly was a good friend, and he ended up
married to grandma and had 4 more children: Jessie, my
mother, Pauline, Irene, and John. Both Linda and her
husband, and Alva and her husband, were farmers.
Mary on the other hand, was not going to marry a farmer
so she went to the big city and got an apartment and a
job in a Linotype shop. She married one of the
operators named Charlie; then later divorced him,
bought the shop, and hired Charlie back to work for her.

She lived in the same apartment, with her daughter, for
40 years. Aunt Alva and Uncle Walt were two of my
favorites. They had three children: Dale, Mabel, and
Claude. Claude was one or two years older than me.
They had twenty acres of Thompson Grapes, and
allowed me to visit with them for two weeks every
summer to work in the fruit and make a little money for
school clothes. My uncle did all his farm work with a
team of huge mules. He was a farmer from the old
school; a farmer's farmer. He never owned a tractor,
and would never let any tractor fumes get on his grapes.
Now on the other hand, a little mule poop made the roots
strong. In his mind God made Thompson Grapes to

make raisins; and none of his grapes would ever be used to make wine. Aunt Alva said it would be a sin and she wouldn't allow it.

Uncle Walt was big and tall, and I never saw him wear anything but bib-overalls. Sometimes they looked like he had them on for weeks, but he filled them out well. He had a gruff way of speaking; but I never heard him say a cuss word, and he would melt when he spoke to Aunt Alva. He liked to tease me because I was not big enough to do the things his two boys could do. He was a strong disciplinarian, one Sunday afternoon we were visiting them and my uncle went to the closet and took out a coiled up black snake and said, "Lets go boys." It seemed the boys had broken up one of his bee-hives, and it was pay back time. I'm sure the boys got the message loud and clear, and it taught me to never mess with Uncle Walt's bee-hives.

Uncle Walt gave me my first dog, a little Boston Terrier, which I named Boots. Boots was a ball chaser, and he went all over on the oil lease looking for someone to throw his ball. But it was to be his downfall as he ended up with no teeth because he used rocks and bricks instead of balls, and burned his eyes from welders' torches waiting for them to throw something.

As I got older, I was allowed to use the mule team more and more. One summer he had a small acreage that he wanted to disk up. I spent my entire two weeks in the seat of the disc plow looking at two big rear ends. I think that was my last summer with them. Well, I'm the only one that I know who doesn't get old as time passes, by but my uncle Walt did grow old. In his later life, he had a very bad stroke, the kind where you linger a long time and then die. Many times Mary and I would take Aunt Alva to visit him at the convalescent hospital, and it would bring tears to our eyes to watch her talk and pet and kiss and hug him without any response back. She felt that he knew that it was her, and she was ready to come back time after time.

Then one Saturday night, we heard that Aunt Alva was in the hospital. Sunday afternoon we went to visit her. When were ready to leave, my aunt said, "Pray for me." I said, "Aunt Alva we pray for you all the time." We left and were walking down the steps of the hospital when Mary stopped mid-way and said, "Do you think she meant to pray for her now?" I said, "I'll pray for her tomorrow when we come back." The next day when we visited they told us that she had suffered a stroke, and was in the same convalescent hospital across the street where my uncle was. We went over there, and she was lying in bed with no response.

I had failed to pray for her on Sunday when she asked. I had to find a time to pray with her. I stopped by Tuesday after I got off work, but still no response. I stopped by Wednesday after work, and still no response. Thursday was the same thing. God I said, "I have to pray for my Auntie and I need your help." Friday after work, I walked in to her room, and there she was propped up in bed with a big smile on her face, and she greeted me by name. I walked over and gave her a kiss. We visited a little while and I said, "Aunt Alva, I need to pray with you." and she said, "good." After I got through she said, "Thank you for that nice prayer."

I left and got into my truck, and cried my eyes out as I said "God, are you trying to tell me that my Spiritual Gift is praying for people?" From heaven I thought I heard, "BINGO YOU GOT THAT RIGHT". My Auntie Alva died peacefully that night. My Uncle Walt, still in a coma for months, died less than a week after her.

To this day, I say that God performed a miracle to help me understand my spiritual gift. Through the years I have tried to be faithful with my gift. I have prayed as soon as I have heard a request, or a nudge from the Holy Spirit. Sometimes the location has embarrassed me, but it's important for me to pray immediately. One Saturday morning, at our Discussion leaders meeting, I was questioned about praying with my men over the telephone. I told them the story of Aunt Alva, and said it was something that I had to do, and that I would step down before I would stop it. I'm sure that somewhere in scripture it says that praying for those in need is a gift that edifies the church.

That's the gift that God gave me.

Chapter Fourteen

AT PEACE WITH GOD

*When we bury someone we love we must bury a part of
our heart. We should not moan this loss. Our hearts,
perhaps, are all that they can take with them.
- Richard Paul Evans*

I believe that it was about 1935 when P.G.&E. bought
out San Joaquin Power Company. A lot of those
employees still worked for P.G.&E. when I came to work.
They were nice people, and I enjoyed working with them.
It seemed that the company had a small piece of
property in the little town of North Fork. The property
was probably acquired during the construction of the
San Joaquin Project. The property also had a spring on
it, and an employee told Indian Mary (a single Native
American mother with many kids that lived on the
adjoining property) she could use the spring for water for
her home, which she did for many years. Now back to
the present time; the adjoining property owner thought
that the spring was on his property, so he filed suit
against Indian Mary for the water she used during the
time that he owned the adjoining property. It was a
sizable law suit and it ended up in court. Indian Mary
immediately got in contact with her old friend from San
Joaquin Power, and the problem fell in to my lap: we had
to survey the property to see who's property the spring
was actually on.

Normally, San Francisco crews would conduct all
property surveys, but they were to busy at this time. I

made a deal with Jack (who was in-charge of surveying in San Francisco) that if he would send just a surveyor with his electronic survey equipment down, I would set-up the triangulation points, and furnish a crew to do all the triangulation work. He could do all the calculations and make the map for the court, and permanently mark the property when he had a crew in the area. The deal was sealed, but could we get it done by the court date?

The next day I rushed to the Madera Courthouse for a copy of the deed. I left Madera and headed for North Fork, along with some maps and information I had pulled from my office. I had a fairly good idea where to look, and sure enough, there in the brush was an iron pipe with a brass cap marked "East 1/ 4 cor. sec. 9"; I had located the monument marking the northeast corner of the property. So I cleared out some brush, and used this monument as my triangulation point "A."

"Where to set the other two points?" I wondered. The forest was dense and blocked me to the West, but everything to the east was clear. Due east was a long bluff, that I thought I could set a second monument for my Triangulation point "B". I took an oiled road through town, and found a gate to a dirt road that would take me out to the edge of the bluff. This was an area where cattle were grazing, so I picked a good spot to drive an iron pipe in the ground for my second Triangulation point. To the Northeast, I spotted a huge rocky area on the side of the mountain, so I drove back into town and took another oiled road that seemed to be headed in the right direction. I drove until I saw a dirt road which I felt might get me near the spot to start looking. Sure enough, walking south I spotted the big flat rock. It was not only what I needed, but it was in a beautiful location.

James William Huckaby
"Mr. Huck"

It had a view of the entire valley below; and because the Sawmill was down that day, the sky was so clear you could almost see the people in town. I found a spot where we could set up our instruments, and drove a cement nail in the rock. I had established my Triangulation point "C", and so headed for home as it had been a long day. The next morning, I called Jack and told him that I was ready whenever he had a surveyor available. I also told him that because the Sawmill would be operating, we would probably have to do the work at night and allow a little extra time.

On Tuesday, the surveyor arrived with all the needed equipment, and at 8:00 pm that night, we left for North Fork. I took two men besides myself as I would have to keep one man at point "B" (because it was in a cow pasture and cows are nosey, they would have knocked down our expensive equipment in no time). We moved the Theodolite (a high powered transit) around to all three points turning all the angles about 6 times. With the electronic distance equipment, we got the measurement of all three sides of my triangle. We shot the North Star for our bearing. Normally we would shoot the sun, but since we were working at night, the North Star was just as good. We used lights and walkie-talkies, and moved tripods to the different points. About three in the morning, we put everything away, and I gave the notes to the surveyor to give to Jack before we headed home. My part was done; or so I thought.

About a week later the San Joaquin employee and I received a subpoena to appear in court the following week. I hoped that the Judge had a map of the final survey because I had not seen one. When we walked in, I could see that he had a map and I relaxed a little bit.

155

He looked at me and asked who I was, and why was I in his court. I told him I was James Huckaby, and that I worked for P.G.&E. as a surveyor, Licensed by the State of California, and I was there if he had any questions about the map. He immediately motioned for me to come up. "Show me the spring and the two pieces of property." I explained the map showing him that the spring was well within the P.G.&E. property. The Judge turned to the party filing suit and said, "I guess you can't sell water that isn't yours. Case dismissed." I thought I heard little Indian Mary say, "Praise the Lord", and so did I.

Now I tell this long tail to show you that my work wasn't always straight forward, and that sometimes I had jobs that made me bite my fingernails. Also, that Triangle Point "C" became my Shangri-La, it was a place that I later went to when I needed to have some time alone with God. It was a bit off the main road, and no one could see my car. A visit there was like a week at church camp, and I used it often. My father died in 1982 from a heart attack while asleep in bed. It was a bit of a shock for me. I knew that he had become a little feeble, but I thought he had a few more years. My mind always drifted back to the hard work we shared building the cabin. I knew that he could drive nails the rest of his life; and he did for many years, but the time finally came when I had to say, "Good bye Dad."

My father was about twenty years old when his father died of pneumonia; he was the oldest of four boys and one girl. The family lived in the small little town of Sanger, and I wouldn't be surprised if Dad was not the sole source of income for the family. I never knew how much education my father had, but I would be surprised if it were more than the seventh grade. He could do his ciphering well enough to pay his bills, but that was about his limit. He was not a good reader, but they took the newspaper just so Mom could do the crossword. In mid-life, my father joined a book club, and when he died he had closets full of books that no one had ever read. I guess he felt that the number of books you had was some kind of a sign of your intelligence. My father was a truck driver by trade, and there was no load that he wasn't willing to accept the challenge. The San Joaquin Power project (which I've already mentioned), was the development my father trucked all the big generators to their power houses for when I was a baby.

My sister Betty arrived in 1926, while we were living in a little house on the east side of Fresno. The depression years were tough for my father to make a living. When he had a job we lived in Fresno, when the job failed he moved the three of us to live in Belridge with Grandma. Once when we were in Fresno, and Dad was working for a trucking outfit, he had a big load going to San Francisco. That day was a treat for me because he took me with him; I remember that trip even to this day. When my grandma Finley died in 1935, Dad got on with the Belridge Oil Company.

My dad got the cabin property late in the summer of 1954. We cleared out the old building down to the ground, and salvaged any of the useable lumber, stacking and covering it. We had a big tree (three foot diameter) that had to be removed so we fell it and sawed it up. When we were done, the ground was ready to start building the cabin the following year. I drew the plans for the cabin, and Dad approved them, and then took them to the Forest Service for approval. Every thing was "go go go", which you will read about in another Chapter coming later for the cabin. We finished the cabin in 1960; it took five years of hard work to complete the job, so my father had twenty-two years to enjoy his hard work.

In the fall of 1981, together we closed the cabin for the winter. He was so happy he spent the weekend doing light work and singing a little song. Little did I realize that this would be his last trip to his beloved cabin. Later, I was so happy that we had that time together, but I struggled to accept that my Dad was gone. He had more nails to drive I thought. The Monday morning after dad's funeral I got my survey crews on their way to work, and left the office headed for Triangulation Point "C". I finally broke down and cried, and was able to release my father back to God. I spent about four hours there that day, and several short visits followed after that for a few weeks.

My mother passed away in 1984, two years after my father, and her passing was a terrible shock for both my sisters, and me. Previously, mother had surprised all of us when she told us she would stay in their home in Bakersfield after dad died. She said she would be all right by herself; after all, she still had dad's 38 hand gun in the little chest beside the bed. No way was she going to live with any of her kids. So Be It. Lois lived in Lodi, while Mary and I lived in Fresno, and two or three times a month one of us would visit mother. Betty would visit mother for a couple of weeks two times a year. And Miss Independent (as I often called my mother) could do her thing.

As I have already written, mother was the oldest of the

Wilson children, but there was little difference in age between mom and my aunt Pauline. In fact, they both were raised on the farm, both graduated in the same year from the same high school, and both were married on the same day in a double marriage ceremony. Mother was always very patient with dad during those depression years. She hated the separation, but knew that she, my sister, and I were getting three good meals at grandmas. When Dad got on with Belridge, she was very happy. It was about 1950 that Belridge decided to build a new two teacher school. The new school would have a cafeteria, and the children would have hot lunches. Mother got on as one of the cooks, and worked there until she retired.

My mother was a real mothers' mother; she was the greatest mother ever. She was beautiful: beautiful to look at, had a beautiful heart, and anything you can think of as beautiful, she had it. I think that she thought every kid needed some kind of dessert after supper. Sometimes it might be one of her beautiful Orange Cakes, or it might be one of her apple pies with the apples ready to pop out. When she passed the pie, Dad always had a piece of cheddar cheese for himself. I always used milk on mine until I grew up and I found that Dad was right; it was better with cheese. She was a cooks' cook.

Mom was the disciplinarian of the family, and she had more than one way to discipline. Dad on the other hand said that he had been "beat on" so many times by his father that he would never lay a hand on his kids; and I think he never did. Mom on the other hand, was kind of handy with the fly swatter, or a swat with a ruler. Our first house at Belridge, Grandma's old house, had two bedrooms with a bathroom between them and two closets back to back. Each closet had a bench across the back to set shoes on. When Betty and I got to fussing, Mom would send each of us to sit in a separate closet on the bench. There were times she would find us fast asleep on that bench. This was her form of "TIME OUT" a long time ago.

As we grew older, mom used a totally different form of discipline; we called it "THE LOOK". The look for me appeared like if I had just shot a little bird with my BB Gun, and it could not fly anymore; how cruel that would be, and it was all my fault. All I could do was run to mother with my arms wide open, hugging her while crying "I'm sorry I'll never do it again." Mother had a way of mending broken hearts; she had three little hearts to mend, and she used a different way for each one. As we grew older, each of us learned our own way to best avoid the look.

As mother grew older, we got to where she and the entire family thought we should sell the house in Bakersfield, and find a Senior Citizen place where she would have good care. We found such a place in the little town of Reedley; run by the Mennonite Church and just about twenty miles from Fresno. We moved mom in and knew she would be well-cared for, and we hoped she would be happy for several years. Not true, in less than a month, mom passed away in the middle of the night from a bleeding ulcer. The entire family could not believe it. How could it be? But she was gone. We got her laid beside dad in the Bakersfield cemetery, and afterward we returned to our homes.

On my first day back to work, by about 10:00am I was

headed again for Triangulation Point "C". I needed to ask God why. Why had he taken my mother so soon? I cried and talked to God, and like my father, I was there until mid-afternoon. I returned several times in the weeks ahead until I finally agreed that they had reached their final goal - they were together once again. Many times, when I felt sad or blue, I would take a run up there for a quick little talk with God. The last time I had sought God was the decision that I made to retire; we had several visits about that. It seemed that at times I argued with God about what was best, but when the decision was made, I stuck with it. Along with the decision of retirement meant I would no longer have access to my Triangulation Point "C"; no longer could I go to my space where I sat on the big flat rock looking out over the peaceful little town of North Fork. I will always be eternally grateful for the opportunity to save Indian Mary's water supply which led to my discovering this refuge from the world, but I had to say good bye.

Not being able to go back when I retired left a vacuum in my soul. Thank you for the weeks and weeks I had such a place where I could commune and find peace with God when I was confused or wounded; looking for answers and divine guidance.

GOOD BYE Triangulation Point "C".

Chapter Fifteen

MY FATHER'S CABIN

"I once read that love is like a rose: We fixate on the blossom, but it's the thorny stem that keeps it alive and aloft. I think marriage is like that. The things of greatest value are the things we fight for. And in the end, if we do it right, we value the stem far more than the blossom."

"A new board begs for a nail."
- Richard Paul Evans

Enjoying Grandpa's Cabin

Off and on in the previous chapters I have mention dibs and dabs of my father's cabin, and I think it deserves a full chapter because it was a very important decision for my parents to make. Years after the cabin was finished, and long after my parents have gone, I'm still uncertain as to where my dad got the money to build the cabin. I have an idea but it's only a guess. My father once told me that Belridge Oil Company had a stock plan for the employees: for every share the employee bought, the company would contribute a half a share. My father told me he had invested in that plan, but at the time of his death, he had no money in it. I have always felt that was where the money came from for the cabin.

Whether it is true or not it makes a good story.

As I write this section you must remember that the beautiful highway 168 that leads from Fresno to Huntington Lake now existed only in someone's dreams back when we started building the cabin. In 1955 the only route to get there was by the dreaded Tollhouse grade: the first challenge for a pick-up and a trailer. Farther up the road was the equally challenging Big Creek grade, which was all second gear work. So when you arrived, you were happy and lucky to be at the cabin site.

All we could think about the winter of 1954 was that we were going to be building a cabin come spring! We knew one thing for sure: whatever we built had to be ready for the snow in the fall. The big question was, would we have the time to get that far? By mid December, Dad had submitted the final plans to the Forest Service and received their approval to build. On Friday, May 6th, Dad loaded up a small borrowed truck and a two wheel trailer with some of the wood from two buildings he had purchased from Belridge Oil Company, and headed for Lot 35 (the future home of our cabin). I was to meet him there early the next morning, and as I rounded a horseshoe turn on the Big Creek grade, there sat the two wheel trailer just off the road; it was just too much for the truck. We unloaded the wood from the truck, and then went down the hill and got the trailer. We then unloaded it, but decided there was too much snow on the ground, and would try again in two weeks.

We met at the site again on the morning of May 21st. Dad brought the rest of the lumber up from his home, and we built the two tent floors for our camp site, and set up both tents. My father made the acquaintance of a noted Huntington Lake builder named Floyd Smith. He proved very helpful during our building experience. He told my father that the tunnel muck and sand at the head of the lake made an excellent cement mix. With Dad's pickup and small trailer, we hauled load after load after load of both for all the cement work. We laid out the building site, and built the foundation forms from the wood we salvaged from the old cabin. The next weekend we began adding our concrete recipe to a small portable electric cement mixer, and began pouring the foundation; the cabin was finally under way. I would mix the concrete, and Dad would pour and tamp; it was a long and hard process that took two full days, but we finally finished and left it to set up for the next weekend. Before we left to go down the hill that Sunday night, Dad said, "I've got some lumber on its way up next Friday."

That next weekend when I drove up the driveway, I had the shock of my life. Standing just off the driveway stood two huge piles of lumber; two full truck loads. My father had gone to a lumber yard in Bakersfield with a copy of the cabin plans, and ordered everything we needed for both the cabin and the garage.

Everything!

Lumber, windows, plumbing, cupboards, the works. I almost passed out because we were definitely committed now; at least a third of those two piles had to go from being horizontal on the ground to vertical before the snow fell; could we do it? We both spent our one month vacations, and every weekend giving it all we had.

Mom became Queen of the cookhouse; she conquered the wood stove and turned out some wonderful food (before the advent of low fat and high fiber). Hot biscuits, cakes, and pies were all easy for her. She always had a nice meal for us.

After weeks of work we finally got the floor down and the walls up. Dad then hired Mr. Smith to help us cut and put up the rafters. Later he would have him shingle the roof as well. At last it was time to put the felt on the outside walls and cover it with boards and bats. We put up the two doors, but time had finally caught up with us, as we weren't able to set the windows. So we made covers for the window spaces, and nailed them to the building. We stored the rest of the cabin lumber, windows, sheetrock, knotty pine, etc inside the cabin. We then placed the garage lumber, shingles and such under the cabin where it would remain for the next two years. We had won the race, and had accomplished everything we had hoped for the first summer (although I'm still not sure how we were able to do it). We took down the tents, locked up the cookhouse and privy, hooked up the trailer, and all went home to wait for the summer of 1956.

We approached 1956 with a completely different frame of mind. The time pressures that first summer had been a constant worry for me, while Dad on the other hand seemed to have no concern. This summer, time wouldn't be so critical, and we could enjoy working at a more relaxed speed.

Over the winter we had wondered how the cabin would hold up under the snow. When we arrived for the first time in the spring, we noticed that the cover on the upstairs bedroom window was ajar. Some one had been in the cabin. We went through the cabin and found everything in tact; nothing damaged and nothing taken. We decided that maybe some one must have needed to get out of a storm and found refuge in our cabin. That sign told us something about the strength of the cabin; if it had snowed so much that someone could walk into our upstairs bedroom window and the cabin was still standing, we had done something right.

We set up the tents and opened the cookhouse. After our camp was reestablished, the first thing we did was to set the windows in place as we pulled the covers off the window openings. Dad hired Mr. Smith again, and with us as his laborers, he put in the rough plumbing. The head electrician who worked for Belridge took a two week vacation at Huntington, and while there he completed the electrical work.

Next we decided to start putting up the sheet rock. During this period of the construction, I asked Dad about the stairway. He said, "Oh Bud, you can take care of that." We still had a lot of 1"x 12" boards left from the old cabin that I could experiment with. I must have cut up a dozen of them before I had the right configuration. I'm sure there is an easy way to cut out stairways, but that is often how the cabin got built, doing it the hard way through trial and error.

The fireplace was built by a elderly man, and his middle aged son from Clovis. It took them two days to complete it. Everyone thought that the fireplace was the most beautiful part of the cabin. When we stopped working that fall, we had all of the sheet rock up, and the flooring in place upstairs. 1956 was an amazing summer: it was a real pleasure to know that every board and every sheet rock panel that went up brought us that much closer to completion. What a joy to see each room taking shape and ready to paint. When we returned to our homes, we had a real sense of accomplishment.

As soon as the snow melted in 1957, we were ready to go again. We had our first real let down that spring. As we drove up the driveway, we spotted the top half of our fireplace chimney lying on the ground. The dormer that we had built to break the snow away from the chimney had been too small to do the job. The effect of the tragedy was greater on our pride than it was on Dad's pocketbook. The top half of the fireplace chimney lying on the ground told the world that the world renowned "Cabin Builders" didn't know as much as they thought! We built another dormer about three times as big as the first one, and then contacted the people in Clovis. The son came up and repaired the brickwork and then we never had another problem with it.

Dad wanted to get the floor tiles down next. He said that next Friday afternoon he would go to Bakersfield and pick up a tile man, and they would go on up to the cabin that night. The man started early Saturday morning and worked until six o'clock that night to finish the job. I never saw a man work as hard as he did; he laid all of the tiles with little help from us.

Most of the summer was spent painting. We completed both downstairs bedrooms, the bathroom, and kitchen. We put up the kitchen cupboards, and brought in the new electric range. In late September on a Sunday night, I had to go home to work the next week. I left Mary and the children with the folks, and as I was ready to drive out the driveway I said, "If you all haven't moved from the tents and cookhouse into the cabin when I return next Friday, I will turn around and go right back to Fresno." When I arrived at the cabin that next Friday, the tents and floors were gone, the privy with the flush toilet had disappeared, and the cookhouse was locked. Mom met me at the door and said, "Buddy, dinner is on the table in the cabin."

What a celebration!!!

1958 would be the year that would bring the cabin to completion. All those long summers, working with a limited amount of time had finally paid off. We had left the knotty pine paneling for the living room as the last project for two reasons: first we wanted plenty of time to complete the living room, and second, we could use the left over pieces to complete the upstairs bedrooms. Our goal was to have this room compliment the beautiful fireplace. Each board was hand chosen for its wood grain and color. Each one that went up had to match perfectly with the one that was already in place. We went through the pile time and time again to get just the right board to match, while all of the rejected knotty pine went upstairs.

My father had purchased a special kind of lacquer that brought out the grains in the wood. The fumes from the lacquer were so strong, we feared for my Mary who was a few months pregnant. I took her back to Fresno, and then returned to help finish up the project. We gave the walls two coats of varnish, and then put up the ceiling tiles. We were quite proud of the way the room finished. Since we had already put up the second floor ceiling tiles the previous summer, all that was left to do upstairs was the knotty pine paneling, two coats of varnish, and the floor.

The inside of the cabin was almost completed at this point, and it was time to start on the outside again. We had the roof and walls to stain, and the front porch to finish. My father chose a forest green for the roof, and a pine bark color for the walls. With a three gallon Hudson sprayer, he gave the roof and walls two coats of paint.

For three summers we had been gathering rocks and dirt for the space where the front porch would be. So now all that was left was to put down a nice layer of cement over the top to finish it. We got out the old cement mixer, a few loads of tunnel muck, and some sand, and finished the porch. We built forms for the garage floor, put in the plumbing for the wash room, and poured the garage floor. We would let the porch and the garage set through the winter, and then finish them up on our return the following spring.

It's the spring of 1959; time to pull off the old wood covers on the windows and doors for the very last time. Before we would leave in the fall, we would have some nice new shutters for them. Spring would be spent putting up the porch rail, and replacing the moldings around the windows since the old wood covers had been nailed into the old moldings all these years. We then applied a coat of paint to both and moved on.

It was time to start on the garage, so each of us took three weeks of our vacation to begin the work. The concrete floor had gone through the winter in good shape; no cracks or breaks. We moved the garage lumber from under the cabin where they had been stored for three years. By mid summer we had the garage all up and stained to match the cabin. We put in the rest of the plumbing, and finished the wash room.

Enjoying Their Labors

My parents retired in 1965, and spent every summer from that time on at the cabin. They loved to take a lunch and go into the back country, and would often go to Ward Lake and fish off the bank. Each year my father would go to the Forest Ranger and get a wood cutting permit. Then he would go into the forest and cut up some old tree that had fallen down. He would come home with a pick-up loaded down with logs so big you wondered how he ever got them into the truck. His theory was a guy couldn't have to much fire wood. If a little was good, a lot was better; and they never ran out. My two sisters and our families enjoyed lots and lots of wonderful times visiting our folks at Huntington Lake during the summers. Both my sisters had much longer distances to travel to get there so they came whenever they could. My parents truly enjoyed our visits, but they also enjoyed the time they spent alone at the cabin.

For The Record

My two sisters and I, and our families, and our family's
children, and their families have always called the cabin,
"Dad's Cabin" or "My Father's Cabin" or "Grandpa's
Cabin." Nothing could be farther from the truth; IT WAS
MOTHER'S AND FATHER'S CABIN.

I am thinking of a story I once heard. It seems that there
were two carpenters working on the roofs of two houses
that were side by side. The one on the left, Bill, noticed
that his friend Sam would pound a nail in the roof and
then throw a nail over his shoulder. Bill watched his
friend repeat this several times. Bill finally asked what
he was doing. Sam's answer was some of these nails
have the head on the wrong end and I can't drive it.
Bill's answer was just save them they are for the other
side of the roof.

I have thought about this story because I believe that
every time Dad drove a nail, the next one he would say,
"This one is for you Mother." Our mother worked over
that hot wood stove cooking three meals for us every
day for years without a grumble; plus a lot of cakes, pies,
and cookies. Our father loved our mother dearly: he
kept her on a pedestal. I would fear for anyone who
ever abused our mother. I have shanghaied my two
sisters to share how they remember how our father
showed his love to our mother.

From Our Memory Chest (by Betty and Lois)

Betty you're up because I got your e-mail first:

"What you are asking for is a little hard, because their

feelings for each other were so constant. They never seemed to be lost for affection for one another. I know that he always bought her a corsage to wear to church on special days, Easter, Mother's Day, etc, and took her out to dinner or brought in when she had spent the day at the beauty shop. AND what about the time she blew up the beans in the pressure cooker? Didn't he show some real love when he washed the kitchen ceiling and walls for her, then took her back to the beauty shop to get all the beans out of her new hairdo? AND didn't she always giggle at all the ornery little tricks that he pulled on us kids? She really thought it was funny when we girls would use his famous powder puff all over our doodads. Many times I have seen him grab her and give her a big kiss and mess up her lipstick. She always cooked his favorite meals. Who else ever ate bread and milk for dinner? AND that good old round steak that she cooked for him, and you and I always tried to be first to, "Kings X" the bone. I also remember the blisters that she had on her heels after going fishing with him. I was always happy that he never took me along. AND our dear Dad ALWAYS opened the car door for our adorable Mother.

When Daddy and Mother would come home from shopping, Dad would walk around with a mysterious bag and a gleam in his eyes. He would dip into it and put something in his mouth. Of course we knew that it was candy, and with slobbers running down to our knees, he would finally turn the candy sack over to us - we didn't get much store candy while we were growing up at Belridge. AND how exciting it was when we wanted to go somewhere for a ride, and Dad always knew a good place to see in the desert - we went to the DUMP. I loved to go there; you always could find something exciting out there. AND Bubble gum- not us kids. Dad would bring home some really great tar, and that was a treat for us. Dad was really good with little white lies, and big ones too, He would fill us full of some great big story, and because we knew better than to believe him, we would turn to Mama and say, "Is that true Mama?" Mama never could lie. She would try, but always got a grin on her face, and we knew that it was another Huckaby fib.

One night we were all at Huntington Lake camped out around our camp fire, when one of us noticed that some people near us had fire on the ropes of their tent. The tent was in real danger, and they were in it. Soooo being brave and helpful Huckabys, we all grabbed a bucket of water and started running to save them. Now as I remember, it was Dad, Lois, Mary, and me. Now mind you it was totally dark, and being as graceful as a flying pig, I fell over a rock; the clatter, bang, and screams would have awakened anyone asleep as far away as Fresno. In fact, I think Bill who was home, thought he was having an earthquake. Anyway after dousing their tent with water, the poor people climbed out and thought they were under attack by crazy people who actually were trying to save their lives - and they didn't even say "thank you". BUT for at least a solid week, Dad never stopped saying loudly, "Fireman, fireman, save my daughter!"
One time the folks came to San Diego to visit us, and we took them to a Charger football game - the Chargers against Buffalo. Mama was real excited because there was a cannon that they shot off every time the Chargers made a touchdown, she waited and she waited because she wanted that canon to shoot. Well there never was a Charger touchdown. I was totally embarrassed and

mad; for at least 30 years every time Dad would think about football, he would ask me, "Betty did the Chargers ever beat Buffalo?" I always silently prayed that no one would bring up the subject of football.

Bless his heart, when I was a teenager, he never once complained that I always had his socks stuffed down into my bra, and he never could find a matched pair in his drawer, 'cause I was wearing the mates. And did I ever look great in that blue LETTERMAN'S SWEATER that belonged to my sweet brother; when he was looking for it, I was wearing it. Then after baby sister got to be a teenager, there went Dad's socks again.

Dad never believed in spanking his kids, and he never did, BUT Dad had the LOOK, and that Look could make you want to crawl in a hole and pull the whole world in on top of you. Nothing was worse than that awful LOOK that could come out of those blue eyes - sometimes I would have rather had the spanking. Dad was a great father: he worked real hard at Belridge and paid his Bills, but he never paid a bill until after there were groceries in the house for his family. AND I knew I was not his favorite daughter, but which ever one of us who happened to have his arms around us would hear him whisper in our ear, "You know that you are my favorite daughter." Sometimes it was Lois or Mary, and sometimes I was the lucky one. We all loved him.

Lois it's your turn:

"I have memories of Mama and Daddy showing affection for each other, it was just such a loving way they had with each other; it was unconditional and everyday the same. It was just something that I always knew: that they loved each other and it was just always there out in the open. To me, Daddy just worshiped Mamma; she was a little bit more reserved and didn't show a lot of emotion. This is my memory anyway; I think she was more private in her feelings, and Daddy just let it all hang out. You could always tell if you were in trouble just by looking into his blue eyes, and boy I would just about wet my pants. I really believe that in heaven Mama and Daddy are living in that cabin, and Daddy is raking pine needles. I do think that we all have different memories of them that we each remember a little differently. I do know that there was always so much love in this family for all of us. To me Daddy was my Rock, and Mama was my Queen.

Do you remember the time that Mama sat on Dad's false teeth when he put them in his pocket and then draped his shirt over Mama's vanity stool, and down she sat on them? Or the time that Daddy was on his hands and knees in their closet looking for a cricket, and Mama threw open the door not knowing he was in there and hit him on the head. Or every time I went out on a date Daddy would leave the toilet seat up and the bathroom dark, and in I would come and go straight to the water, I would cuss and he would laugh.

Or I would be taking a bath at night and he would turn of all the lights, pitch dark and me in my birthday suit. Every time Mama cooked anything we would have to wait for Daddy in the bathroom. When he came out he would always have water dripping off the hair on the back of his head.
Daddy always had what he thought was his own powder puff; what he powdered I don't know. But I do know Mama, Betty, and maybe Mary, and myself used that

powder puff on us (and I mean everywhere) and he never knew.

I remember so many fun things: like every time we went somewhere we would just about get back to the house and I'm just bursting to go pee and all of a sudden Daddy would holler Kings X on the toilet. I'm hurting and Mama would always stick up for Daddy, he said it first so you'll just have to wait. AND how many times did Margaret tell Daddy, "George your pants are unbuttoned," and Mama would just sit there like a little queen and Daddy would say, "Oh I didn't know, ha." He did it every time Margaret came over.

Remember how serious Mama was about the wrestling matches? Daddy would take her to Bakersfield to see them once a week - and boy you better not try to tell her they were fixed either. AND how many times did he take Mama and I to Buttonwillow and then catch me off guard somewhere while I was shopping and start singing, "Those Oklahoma Hills Where I Was Born"; he just about embarrassed me to death with that song. Now, what a hoot, I'm living in those Oklahoma Hills. He would always say if he saw a car with a mattress on top of it, it was Okies moving, but if it had a couple of mattress's, then they were rich Okies.

One time they came to see us in Woodbridge when the kids were teens, and George always wore that old ratty sock cap on his head at night trying to make his hair straight. One night we were going out to supper, and Daddy had stuck that ratty old cap in his pocket. After we ate and everyone stood to leave, Daddy suddenly pulled that old thing on his head: his ears were sticking straight out and he says to me don't worry honey, I'll help you out of here. I just about fainted, looked around for Mama, and she was nowhere in sight - how she got out of the restaurant so fast I will never know, but she did have a lot of practice.

One year for Christmas they were spending it with us and I got handed this most beautiful little box. I opened it and inside was Daddy's big toenail that he had smashed and come off his toe; and I got it for Christmas. Then on one of Mother and Dad's camping trips, we all heard about Dad getting a red hot coal in his boot. Well from the way the story from Mother went, he yelled and screeched, and danced a most wonderful jig around the camp site. Mother found it ever so funny, laughed her head off until he was finally able to remove the boot and get the awful thing out. No help from Mama, she just sat back and enjoyed the show. Mama had a great sense of humor, HA. (BABE - A NEW DANCE WE MUST TRY THE NEXT TIME WE DANCE TOGETHER)

After Daddy died, Bob and I went down to see momma and she decided she wanted to go to the funeral home and pick out her casket - so off we went. When we got in the room with all the caskets I spot a pink casket exactly like Daddy's blue one was, so I take her over there and show her. "Look Mama, here's one exactly like Daddy's." She picks up the tag with the price and says so stern to me, "Well, Lois, the blue one costs more than the pink one does and that will never do for Daddy's to cost more than mine." And that is why she got buried in a blue one exactly like Daddy's was - at the same price.

Saying Goodbye

In the winter of 1981-1982 my father had some problems with his eyes and couldn't drive anymore. He had cataract surgery, but it was not successful. Late in the summer I drove to Bakersfield to pick up dad and the two of us went to the cabin for the weekend alone. It was his first trip to the lake that year, and he seemed so happy to be there. The whole weekend he went around humming a little tune - I had never heard him do that before. I watched him through the kitchen window looking at the blue jays flying around. I watched him replacing the rocks that had been moved along his pathways. Saturday afternoon we were sitting on the porch looking down toward the lake reminiscing, and Dad said, "Bud, we really did it up right, didn't we?" I replied, "Dad, I think we just about created a miracle." I had no idea at that time that my father would never visit his beloved cabin again. He passed away on March 13th of 1983. Mother followed two years later almost to the day.

I will close this chapter with a letter written by my father's nine year old great granddaughter.

Huntington Lake

As I look at him surrounded by the oak tree that once hovered above, for a moment, I too die. I cry continuously, feeling as though I'll never stop. As I look at him, I recall all of those special memories that no one can ever erase, not even my nine year old mind. I remember it vividly, as though it were only yesterday.

We arrived at Huntington Lake. I awoke to find our car

enwrapped by gigantic, green trees hovering above their newly arriving guest. I got out of the car and could hear the rustling of the leaves as the wind gently blew them from side to side. The air was fresh and clean…..a tremendous difference from the smog-filled city I left only hours behind. As we walked to the cabin, pebbles crunched beneath my feet. My grandparents came out to meet us. Warm, enthusiastic hello's were exchanged and lemonade was poured. We sat on the porch conversing about how well they looked and how big my sister, Shelly had gotten. At nine years of age, this was not a very stimulating topic. Grandpa Huckaby sensed my boredom, and asked whether Shelly and I would like to tour Huntington Lake. Curiosity sparked, we were on our way.

Walking down the rocky road on the way to the "General Store", I found myself relating to "Where the Red Fern Grows." All I was missing were my dogs. The general store was exactly that……. GENERAL. It had basic necessities: milk, bread, canned goods, and of course, candy, and soda (bottled not canned). This definitely wasn't VON'S, but it was neat. Grandpa Huckaby bought each of us a soda. We drank our sodas as we walked the dirt road which lead is to the lake.

Then, as well as now, I've yet been unable to find accurate words to describe this lake's beauty. The water was crystal clear and azure blue. The blinding sun shown down, creating sunbeams reflecting off the water.

On our walk back to the cabin, we saw flowers of yellow and orange. Grandpa Huckaby picked a handful. He handed my sister and me a couple of flowers a piece. Back at the cabin, we ate dinner. Exhausted after a long day of excitement, I went to bed. I awoke early next morning to a worm amber colored fire and a good breakfast. Anticipating the day to follow, I curled up in Grandpa Huckaby's green recliner, wishing I could stay forever. But, as I grew and learned, I found that nothing stays forever.

And now, four years later, I found myself no longer enclosed by beautiful full trees and warm glowering sunlight. I shivered from the bone chilling cold. The beautiful lake I remembered became a stream of tears. That sweet caring man, who led the lake tour and bought the pop, lived no more……… No one can live forever, but truly special people leave this world embedding wonderful memories that continue to live in our hearts, our memories, and our stories. It had rained throughout the church service. It almost seemed as though God too was crying over our loss. Leaving the church to go to the burial site service, a colorful rainbow suddenly brightened the sky.

God had taken over now!! Grandpa Huckaby is in his own log cabin where no fire wood is needed, and dirt roads lead to eternal happiness. After witnessing close friends and family lowering him into the ground and covering his casket with dirt, I placed a small handful of yellow and orange flowers on the mound just to let Grandpa Huckaby know that I was remembering………And would always remember the special unforgettable memories he created for me.

BY KIMBERLY D. GILES,
Our Betty's Granddaughter

Our Created Miracle

Chapter   Sixteen

SNIPPETS AND LEFT-OVER'S

"I have learned that the simple acts of kindness
may have profound consequences;
though more likely for the giver than the recipient."

"The weather is always fair when people are in love."
- Richard Paul Evans

It is the summer of something (I don't remember when),
but all of our gang were going over to Redwood
Christian Park for a week of Church Camp. Bill and
Carol were both off work, and Sue was working at the
camp that year. It also might have been the year that
Mary phoned us during camp to tell us that Kristy was
born, and Butch, Jim, and I wore our Grandfather's shirts
the whole week long.

The time wasn't important but what happened was. It
was mid afternoon that Mary and I were just relaxing on
a bench, taking in a little of that mountain sunshine,
when up walked our new Pastor, Al VomSteeg, and Rob
Lyness. Rob and Lynda were one of our young married
couples at the church, and were both about Bill's age. I
thought I learned how to handle Al when he first became
the Pastor. Once I casually suggested that I thought we
needed a couple of handicapped parking spaces, and he
replied, "When do you want to do it?" I never ever
suggested anything else to him after that. Al shot right
from the hip, no fooling around. So I expected
something was coming, he hadn't just walked up to
shoot the bull. Here it came; "We want you and Mary to

sponsor the Young Married Couples in the church."
POW, POW, a bomb shell just like that. I was just about
to retire and told myself I was not going to get involved in
church stuff; just relax and take easy for a while. But I
asked him to let us pray about it, and we would have an
answer for him by the end of camp. We spent much of
the rest of camp with Rob and Lynda, and learned to
love them both. By the end of camp there was only one
way to reply: we would be the new sponsors for the
young married couples group.

The next 3 or 4 years were one of the greatest times of
our lives. When it all started, Mary and I were a little bit
surprised to find that the Young Married Group consisted
of one and a half couples. I say a half because the
second couple, Bruce and Margie made a habit of
coming to about every other meting. Bruce owned a
struggling business that required a lot of his time. First
to join the group was Bill and Patty and their 2 year old
son Roger (Roger tended to be the big interest in the
group meetings). Next to join the group was Ken and
Karen, and then Bill and Connie. They came in just as
new comers to the church; part of our church growth
(Pastor Al brought in a lot of new faces). Then Gary and
Ann joined, friends of Bill and Cathy, who had been in
the East somewhere while Gary was going to school.
Then Walter and Karen from Canada, and a couple with
two little children from Kansas who were going to the
Mennonite Seminary at Pacific College joined. Also from
the Seminary were Michel and Jeanie who were
studying to be religious counselors.

Michel was a very unique person in many ways. He was
a quadriplegic, and had a smile that was glued on his
face whenever you saw him. He and Jeanie had a van

that automatically moved his big electric wheelchair in and out, and placed him on the ground. He had what looked like a small table in front of him where his hands lay. Between his hands was a fair sized bible, and on the corner of the table were two sticks about one foot high with something that looked like a eraser on its end. He could reach to the corner of the table, and with his mouth pick up one of the sticks to flip open his bible and find a scripture faster than anyone else in the group. He was truly a man of God, his faith, and his witness were wonderful. He was a great blessing to everyone who knew him.

I don't remember how it happened that our group got the use of a cabin at Bass Lake. The muscle guys were trying to get Michel and his big chair into the house, and on about the third attempt little 100 pound Jeanie said, "Get out of the way." In about 30 seconds she had the chair in the house. We truly had a great weekend: the girls had lots of food, we had a nice fireplace each night, and a row boat to use. Each evening we had a time of Bible study with the group, followed by a time of individual sharing. When the time came to leave we all just let Jeanie handle the big chair; that seemed to be the fastest way to take care that.

The group elected Walter to be their leader. He would have charge of the meetings; do the lessons and kind of run things. This was great with Mary and I since we didn't feel we were there to run things, we were there to support the group and help with any problems if they had any. Like when Al thought he had some special chore in the church that he wanted to take Walter from the group to do. Rob and I got all hot about it, and went marching into Al's office and told him he couldn't take Walter from the Young Married Group. Al laughed at us and said he would find someone else.

The group heard of a Marriage Seminar up in the General Grant area that they would like very much to attend. The fee to attend was quite expensive, so I offered to make a large stained glass piece. We would hang it in the church and sell tickets for a drawing to make a little cash. So we made up a batch of tickets and the next Sunday morning the guys were ready to start selling when Al told Gerry that we couldn't sell them. One of the major contributors to the church had complained that selling tickets and having a raffle was gambling, and it had to stop. Well stop we did, but not to be totally defeated, we put the glass piece up as a silent auction and made $125.00 for it. But I questioned if what we had originally planned was really gambling, and did it really make a any difference.

Money for the Seminar had to be in by a certain date, and with the $125.00 we made it on time. About two weeks before the Seminar, Michel and Jeanie decided they would like to go, but it was too late to get them in, so Mary and I put them in our place and they got to go after all.

As the group grew and the kids started to become parents, it was total joy for Mary and I to get to love everyone there. Ken and Karen were the first to bring a baby girl into the group. Mary and I went with Ken to bring Karen and the baby home from the hospital, and also stood with them when they dedicated their baby to the Lord. Bruce and Margie were next with a little boy.

After about three years, Mary and I retired from work

and bought a little mobile home in Salem, Oregon, where we spent our summer months. It was time for Mary and I to resign from the group we loved so much. Another couple sponsored the group the next year, but after that the group seemed to just disappear. Later in the year I saw Michel in church by himself, and asked him about Jeanie. He told me that she had left him, and that he was going back to Canada. That was the last time I saw either of them.

Bill and Patty moved to a home in the mountains. Bill and Connie moved to Texas because of his work. Bruce and Margie, Ken and Karen, and Gerry and Ann, all moved to different churches. The Kansas kids moved back to Kansas, Walter and Karen moved to Canada to pastor a church there. Mary and I will always be eternally grateful to Rob and Lynda for asking us to join with them and their dream to start a young married group. To the best of my knowledge they are still doing the Lord's work in the same church. They and all the other couples along with their children, that we met and loved, have truly been a blessing in our lives over the years.

It is very possible that some of the names in this spiritual writing might be incorrect, and if you have found one please take special note of the following:

> "As I get older, it is easier to be positive. I care less about what other people think. I don't question myself anymore. I've earned the right to be wrong."

About six years ago I received word that Michel had died. In the back of my mind it seems that it was an automobile accident, but that is not what is important. What is important is that the world lost a true Man of God. In his severely handicap way, one of his smiles would melt your heart. His eyes showed a heart full of love. I consider it a great honor to have known him for the short period of time I did.

END OF SNIPPET ONE AND START OF NUMBER TWO

It is strange how in my life I have met so many, many people, but can only remember a few. In Navy boot camp, with a barracks full of men, there is only one man whose name I remember. Three years aboard a ship with 100 men, and there is only a hand full that I remember their names or faces. 37 years of work at P.G. & E. and possibly a few more people I can recall. But there are also many people that made a great impression on my life. People who love with the love of Jesus Christ. People who have shared that love with me, and my family over the years. These are the kind of people that pop into my mind when I am wondering what to write about next. Two of these people were Jerry and Lorena Caroll. You might remember this same Jerry I mentioned in an earlier chapter who was in Bible Study Fellowship with me, as well as being a great tennis player. His wife Lorena was one of the greatest prayer warriors that our church ever had. Anyone who had a problem, or needed a shoulder to cry on was just a phone call away. Lorena would answer, "Shall we pray about it?", and then offer a few words of council if she felt the Lord led her that way. She wasn't one to give up on a problem; she would continue to follow up with prayer and council until there was resolution.

One night I got a phone call from Lorena, and she told me there was a certain family in the church that was having some marriage problems, and that the Lord wanted me to go talk with the husband. "Lorena," I said, "I hardly know this man, he'll tell me to go mind my own business." Lorena said, "Jim, get busy about the Lord's work". Which I did only because I knew that she would be praying for me.

The husband and I became the greatest of friends in the future. Lorena was so happy that she called me two more times with the same problem, and I responded by doing just what she told me to do because I knew that it was straight from God.

Lorena had a very dear friend who's name was Mary, and between the two of them they just about took care of all the children's Sunday School Classes. Believe me when I say, the children who were in their classes really learned the word of the Lord. I can verify that because my children went through both of their classes.

Lorena was constantly doing the Lord's work. I saw her lead a lady to the lord in the middle of a bible study class. Whoa, stop the class, the Lord has another believer.

Lorena grew old just like the rest of us, (I think that she was a few years older than Mary and I), but their children were much older than ours were. The last time I saw her, her daughter had brought her to church. I gave her a big hug, and when I did she opened her bible up and pulled out a piece of paper. She handed it to me and said, "Jim, my mind no longer remembers names. This is a list of the people I now pray for." I walked out of the church with tears in my eyes. A year or two later I heard of her passing, and I thought how great it was that in my life I got to know and love a true SAINT. Thank you Lord for bringing her into my life.

END OF SNIPPET NUMBER TWO AND START OF NUMBER THREE

"There is no confection so sweet as a joyful reunion"
- Richard Paul Evans

It has been my experience that sometimes strange things happen in a bible study. Back in the 70's, three dear couples (Jim and Jeanette, Butch and Shari, and Doug and Betty), along with Mary and I, decided to start a Sunday evening Bible Study on the book of James. Years later, some very good bible teachers came from that group, but that first night everyone looked at each other asking what to do, who would do what, and where to start. That night we were at Doug and Betty's home, and we just opened our bibles and read a little, and then talked about it a little. Then we had some coffee and pie, and decided that we would meet the following Sunday night at Butch and Shari's home and would change homes each Sunday. Would you believe that it took us a whole year to complete the book of James, and would you believe that this group studied together for the next 10 years?

A life long bond developed between that group that is still active today.

In the first SNIPPET I had a quote that said, "At my age I had the right to be wrong." So there was a lady in our church that had a son who I will call Bob. He had a very serious illness that kept him bedbound. We heard that she wished someone from the church might visit him from time to time. Doug, Jim, Butch, and I took on the challenge, and we decided that of the four of us, two would be sure to visit Bob once a week. We would visit some, have a scripture reading, and a prayer. Bob had a older brother named Larry, and he kind of made fun of our visits. He made us feel that we were not all that welcome, but we hung in there with our visits. Bob finally passed away, and at his funeral Larry praised us and thanked us for the time we had spent with his brother. What was this? That was not the Larry we knew.

To this day I never knew how or when Larry and his wife came to the Lord, but they did, and they wanted to join our group. We welcomed them with open arms, and after a few meetings, Larry decided he wanted to be baptized by immersion, and he wanted Butch to do it. Larry was a big man, and Butch asked me to help him. One Sunday night, at Betty and Doug's home, in their backyard swimming pool, the three of us got into the pool and baptized Larry. A short time after that, Larry and his wife moved to another church and we soon lost contact with them.

As a group we did lots of things together: picnics, pot-lucks, visits to other churches, a couple of Bill Gather concerts, and we always went to Redwood Christian Park Family Church Camp. I suppose there were those that said we had a click, but the fellowship that developed was like no other. Every year in some way, Sheri gathers all of us together for dinner somewhere. A few years ago when our house in Fresno sold and we were in the midst of moving, Shari got all the gang to our house along with Chinese food that we ate on paper plates. It was one of the best times we had ever had together.

Very Dear Friends

END OF SNIPPET NUMBER THREE
AND START OF A LEFT-OVER

It's the morning of September 18, 2010. Tim and Carol are here, and the four of us are going to Fresno for the wedding of Bill and Cathy's oldest son Josh to Karen. These two kids met at a church camp about 4 years earlier. It was while Josh was at Moody Bible College in Chicago. Josh graduated in 3.5 years, and had been a youth pastor for about a year at Flipside Church in the Madera Ranchos. Karen on the other hand is graduating from Pacific University in Fresno. She wants to continue further studies at the University, and Josh will continue further studies at a later date. At 11:30, Carol had arranged a lunch meeting with the group at a restaurant. Jim and Jeanette were away at a football game, but Butch and Shari, and Doug and Betty were there. What a joy to be with these great friends again. All six of them are still working and in good health. God has indeed been good to all of them. Sheri had breast cancer, and Jim had prostate cancer and back surgery; but they are fine now. I really never could figure out how come they allowed an old man like me to be part of such a wonderful younger group.

We had to be at the wedding site at 3:45 for family pictures, so we went back to the motel to get dressed. The wedding started at 5:30pm, and Karen made a most beautiful bride - she makes my second grand daughter by marriage (Teddy's Julie was the first). They both are the love of my life. Josh was very handsome in his tux. He looked very much like his Dad (a little shorter), and reminded me also of Bill and Cathy's wedding years ago. Well what more can I share, it was one of the most beautiful weddings I have ever seen, and yes I cried a little bit too!!

LEFT-OVER NUMBER TWO

I was peacefully setting in the front row of the wedding waiting for someone to say, "Grandpa, we are ready for some more pictures." All of a sudden a tall man sat down beside me and said, "Remember me?" I looked and looked and had no idea who he was. Finally he said, "I'm John." It was Bill's life long very, very best friend who had driven all the way from Modesto to attend the wedding. It had been years and years since I last saw John. I believe it was when John was still working for the Fresno Bee, and lived in Madera. Tim and Bill were in Fresno, and the four of us played Golf at a Madera

Golf Course. You haven't lived until you played golf with this group. As I recall it was in the dead of winter, cold and foggy, so you had to yell to the next group when you left the green. I cherished the time I spent with the three of them, and I loved John just as I loved Tim and Bill.

Oh if I could just live those twenty or so years over again.

When John was growing up his parents separated and finally divorced. I know that this was a terrible hurt for John, and even as we talked that day, I thought I could sense that things were still not right in his relationship with his father.

During those years when John and Bill were always together, I tried to show John the same love I had for Bill, but I knew I couldn't take the place of his own father. I decided the thing to do was to pray a lot, and try to be there if he needed me. We made our home open to John all through his youth. John left The Fresno Bee after he passed Bar, and went to work at the District Attorney's Office in Madera County, and then later in Modesto for the Stanislaus County District Attorney's Office.

When we spoke at the wedding he said he was handling a murder case. Is this the same boy who came over whenever Bill got a new pair of shoes, and then went home wearing Bill's old ones just like they were new ones? I am very proud of both these men. John has spent his life taking care of his sick mother; Bill and Cathy have given me four great grand sons. I wish I could take some of the credit for their success, but I think they got what they have the hard way----work. If you ever run into either of them, ask them to share the night they tried a little whisky.

JUST A SMALL LEFT-OVER NUMBER THREE

Want to toss this little item in because the time is right. Sue and Randy spent a couple of half days with us while we were staying at The Vintage, and we had a great visit. My father had a joke he played on his daughters Mary, Betty, and Lois. Which ever one happened to be out of hearing range to the other two, he would sneak up to her and say, "You're my favorite daughter." Before the evening was over, he had said that to all three. I could do that to whoever happened to be here, but it wouldn't be true because I love all four equally.

Thanks so much for stopping by Sue and Randy.

In Second Samuel 6:16, David, over the joy of returning the Ark to Jerusalem, was leaping and dancing before the Lord.

Today Mary and I danced for the joy of visiting loved ones.

Chapter Seventeen

THE CRUISE AND THE CHURCH

"Begin at the start, end at the end.
It's the best advice I could give a friend."
- Richard Paul Evans

The Cruise:

It was late 1942, or early 1943, on my second trip into Pearl Harbor that I heard about a religious service at a small outdoor chapel the following Sunday morning. I decided to go by myself, and see what it was all about. I was ready to step onto the gangway when I saw Cham, a friend and fellow radar man, running up the other way. He yelled, "Where you going?" So I told him. He said, "Wait, I'll go with you." I said, "Cham, you just got back from Catholic services; this isn't for you. What would your mom say?" He happily responded, "That's OK, she don't know, and it will get me off the ship for a couple more hours. Just wait."

Cham was only about five tall, and is what I called a white Italian. Cham was Italian, but you'd never know it with his fair skin, blond hair, and blue eyes. The only way we knew that he was Italian was to be around at mail call when he opened his box from his mother with all the Italian food, meats, and cheeses. Hold your nose. On our first trip to Pearl Harbor, Cham went into Honolulu, where he had a few too many drinks. He then went to a tattoo parlor, and got a tattoo of the ugliest sailor girl I ever saw. I had the gang-way watch that night, so I watched as he staggered up the gang-way.

He was so happy I could hardly get him in bed. What a surprise he had the next morning: besides the big head, he took a lot of kidding about his sailor girl.

I had another Italian friend aboard named Herb. Herb was our mailman, and was about the only man that could leave the ship when we were in port. Herb was what I called a black Italian. He had dark skin, deep dark eyes, and both he and Cham were from New York. Herb was married, and had a three year old little girl. In fact when we were in Seattle, he brought his wife back with him from New York, and we stayed at the same hotel and had some very good times together. BUT at the first of the month, when it was time to pay-off my pinochle debt, it was, "Here you go, black Dago" and, "Here you go, white Dago"; there went all my money.

Boy did I get off the track. Cham and I went to the open air chapel that Sunday, and it was a long way from any religious meeting I ever saw; I wished that I had not gone. But as Cham said, it got me off the ship for a couple of hours. There were no religious services aboard ship. In fact, with the exception of when we were in Pearl, of the three years I spent in the Pacific, I was off the ship only two times.

The first time I got off the ship was after we left Tarawa. We needed fuel, and pulled in beside a huge big military tanker to fill up. We were all hooked up taking on fuel, but the water was pretty rough and we were listing a lot due to the anchor of the fuel line. Our captain was concerned the ship would be pulled over so he stood beside the hose with a fire axe. The Captain of the oil tanker yelled over, "DON'T CUT THAT HOSE!" With the rough seas, eventually our ship listed to about 55 degrees, and WACK went the axe. The hose was gone, and we were free of the Big Naval Ship. No more fuel for us. We went back to Makin Atoll to patrol for Japanese subs. Two weeks later, we were recalled to Pearl Harbor, but needed more fuel to make the journey. On our way back we pulled into the little atoll of Johnston Island that was about 750 miles west of Hawaii. On December 29, 1934, President Roosevelt transferred control of Johnston Atoll to the U.S. Navy to establish an air station. In 1936, the Navy began to develop a seaplane base, an airstrip base, and refueling base.

We were the largest U.S. Military ship (300 feet long, 30 feet wide) to enter the Atoll, and had to have a pilot to get us in and out. When we got there, we found a group of Navy Seabees that had been there since way before the bombing of Pearl Harbor, and were crying to go home. They were so glad to see us that our Captain kept only those of us needed to do the refueling aboard, and the rest of the crew was allowed to run free on the atoll and make new friends. This was the first time I got off the ship, and we were welcome to everything on the island, including free rides in the three military tanks that were on the ends of the runway.

The second time that I got off the ship was the Atoll of Ulithi, which was one of the Caroline Islands of the western Pacific Ocean. It was 103 miles east of Yap; an island held by the Japanese where they occasionally launched attacks on Ulithi. Ulithi was a major U.S. Navy base during the war. The Japanese established a radio and weather station there early in the war, and had used the lagoon for anchorage of their ships; Ulithi lagoon was capable of holding up to 700 vessels. Ulithi was perfectly positioned to act as a staging area for the

Philippines, Formosa, and Okinawa. During September 1944, a United States Army regiment landed unopposed, and they took control of the island. A few months later, 617 U.S. military ships gathered in the lagoon for the Okinawa operation. Ulithi was the farthest west we ever got, and the closest to Japan our escort duty required.

The Navy had set up a small recreational area on Ulithi for the Navy crews that had an excellent beach area, a few palm trees, baseball, football, swimming, and just roaming about. So with one third of the crew and two bottles of beer for each man, we spent about three hours there.

Now I never did know the entire story about the beer, but I'll tell you what I heard. The beer was stored in the ship's locker for special occasions. When they went to the locker to get the beer to take ashore, they discovered quite a quantity had disappeared. The Chief, as we called him, was a second class boatswain mate, and he held the key to the locker. Chief was regular Navy, and a full blooded American Indian. Well, not to embarrass the Chief anymore, I will tell you that he lost the key to the locker, and a stripe or two off his arm. But he didn't care because on the coming pay day he would get even as he was the greatest crap shooter aboard ship.

Another thing happened that day, and this next event is worth a few minutes. The war in Europe was over, and we were getting a few of the smaller British ships in the area; one was using the Atoll the same day we were. They were all in swim suits, and their uniforms were all lined up in a row in nice little piles; just like how fireman have their clothes ready to jump in on alert. So when we were all lined up for morning muster the next day, here comes Peter, one of our seamen, walking up in a complete English uniform. He had taken an entire pile of some ones clothes. Even the shoes fit him perfectly. Those two occasions were the only time in probably two years that I left the ship. The only people who did get off were those who handled supplies, and the mailman.

The Church:

The year is 1957, Carol will soon be two years old, and we are settled in at our new home in Fresno. One day we got a visit from Uncle John and Aunt Mary (Uncle John had helped us in finding housing in the past). During their visit, they happened to tell us that they were going to a church in our neighborhood. This was a bit of a surprise to us because I didn't know that Uncle John was a church going person. Good for him I thought, but then they invited us to go with them next Sunday. After gave a few hems and haws, they said they had joined St. Luke's Methodist Church, about a three blocks away from our home. Before they left, we agreed to meet them there the following Sunday. In the early or mid-1940's, a group of Methodists bought a Quonset hut from the army, and set it on the west side of their property - that later became St. Luke's Methodist Church. When we visited the church in 1957, they had moved out of the Quonset hut, and had built a large concrete block sanctuary with a two bedroom parsonage.

Three months later, Mary and I joined the church. The pastor then was T. Elmer Smith who was later replaced by Lynn Haver. Lynn was born in Norway, and he and his family stayed at St. Luke's for about four years.

During his pastorate, the church built a beautiful new sanctuary, bought a new parsonage, removed the old parsonage, and replaced it with a new parking lot; the old church became the Fellowship Hall. After the new church was completed, Lynn Haver, left the church, and Harold Colman preached the first service in our new church.

In 1959, our little Connie passed away and Harold handled the funeral service for us. It was at this time that Mary and I decided to stop playing church and totally give ourselves to serving the Lord. Mary started teaching a Sunday school class for four year old children, while I took on the job of Sunday School Superintendent.

We took on everything asked of us, and enjoyed every minute of it, and Bill, Carol, Sue, and Mary were all very involved in the youth work. Family Church Camp at the Redwood Christian Park every year. It was about this time that I started Bible Study Fellowship, which I loved. Our church had a number of excellent pastors during that time. I thought of St. Luke's as my second church home, and I loved it (since the age of eleven, I always said that my grandmother's church was my first church home).

Sometime in 2000, a big bomb fell - one of our local Methodist Churches, along with about twenty other Methodist churches decided they would perform a Gay Marriage in a Sacramento Methodist Church, and the California-Nevada Conference Bishop condoned it as a Marriage. St Luke's Church, along with six other Methodist Churches believed it to be non-biblical, and withdrew from the Conference.

That's when things got real nasty!

The Methodist Conference said they owned the church and the property, and that we could either buy it back or rent it from them. The members of the church said that they owned it, and that every stick of wood on the property belonged to them; after all, they bought and paid for every bit of it. Some of the other churches were moved off of their properties. One of the churches had their young Pastor and his wife moved out of their church and parsonage, and right onto the street. Not St Luke's, we took the Methodist Conference to court in what turned out to be a long battle. For about a year it seemed that every Sunday we were taking up collections for Attorney's fees. In the end, the court ruled against us, and we lost the case. But we would appeal the ruling, and fight back. It returned to court with lot more lawyer's fees ahead to be paid.

About this time Mary and I were attending a bible study, when one night a couple who were Cameroon Missionaries visited the study. They were bible translators, and Mary and I had sent them support for a number of years. They had two little children and another on the way. They showed us their humble little home, and lots of things about their mission that made our hearts go out to them. The little bit that we had been sending them we were sure didn't go very far. Mom and I talked and prayed about it, and decided that we had given our last support for attorney fees and gifts to St. Luke's. We would take that money and send it to the Kids in Cameroon until they got back on their feet in the mission fields. We would also say 'good bye' to St Luke's, and would seek out another church.

In 2003 we visited the Grace Church of the Nazarene in Fresno. On our first Sunday we found the church in the process of selecting a new pastor, and listened to Carl preach his "get to know me" speech. Later, the church accepted him as their new pastor. We liked Carl immediately, but a good bit of the people did not. As with most change of pastors, a good many people left the church.

The church also had Christian school, grades 1 through 8, that was struggling and looking for new leadership. Carl hired a new man for the position that was put in charge of the school. So some more unhappy members left the church. The church signed for a loan to pay off a school debt, but it continued to struggle, and a short time later they closed the school - leaving this now small church with a debt that they are still paying off to this day.

So when we joined the church we soon discovered it was not a healthy church. Membership was declining, not gaining. Carl was having difficulties keeping everyone happy; I truly liked Carl and tried to show him lots of friendship and love. We were welcomed into the church, and in a short time we made some very close friends: Delmar and Flo, Dude and Ester, Bob and Pauline, Bob and Leona, Glenn and Mildred, Hershel and Louise and Elmer and Joanna. After Sunday morning services, we would all gather at Taco Bell for lunch. Then at 6:00 Sunday night, we met at Bob and Pauline's house for bible study.

This group was not only very special to us, but they were the people who kept the church going financially, and by attendance. We fellowshipped with this group from 2003 until we moved in 2009. When it came time to leave Fresno I had no problem saying good-bye to the old house, but it almost destroyed me to say good-bye to these friends. I have said good-byes a lot of times in my life; but I cannot help but wonder how many of those good-byes were forever, and how many will only be temporary - until we meet together in heaven. I am told that over half of the men in my high school graduating class never returned from the war. How many are waiting for me in heaven?

Spooky, huh?

During the six years our group was together, Delmar, Louise, Hershel, and Glenn went on to meet the Lord. Mary and I, and the rest of the others (now numbering ten) are just waiting for our call.

About eighteen months after Carl started his new position at the church, he took a one year medical leave of absence. The Nazarene church provided a temporary Pastor named Ken to take his place. But when Carl did not return, Ken became Grace's permanent pastor. I talked with Bob the other day, and he said that the church had dropped to about 65 people attending; a drop from nearly 300 when Mary and I first joined. He said that the church rents the old school facilities to a charter school, and that their rent is the only thing that takes care of their finances.

When we moved to Lodi, Bill, Cathy, and their boys were attending the Crossroads Heartland Nazarene Church; right next door to the Vintage where we were living. But we decided that no church could put up with two families of Huckabys, so we decided to shop around a little. First we tried Temple Baptist Church, about a half mile from our home. We went about three times, and decided that it was too large for us with probably 1000 plus members; to big to get comfortable. Some friends here at the Vintage told us about their church – Lodi Avenue Baptist Church, a Southern Baptist, with a membership of a little over a 100; just about our size. We have attended for five years, and eventually transferred our membership there.

Some people store up treasures on earth: houses, cars; "stuff", and every day they move further from their treasure. Then there are people who have stored up their treasures in Heaven, and every day they move one step closer to their treasure. One day closer to leaving this lobby, and entering the main ballroom; and the final dance.

D.L. Moody said in his dying days, *"Some day you will read in the papers, 'D. L. Moody of East Northfield is dead.' Don't you believe a word of it! At that moment I shall be more alive than I am now."*

Chapter Eighteen

THE ANNIVERSARY

*"Tonight Mary fell asleep in my arms I'm not sure
that heaven could be anything more than that."*

*"How sweet is the rapturous state
of soft passions in a heart full of love"
- Richard Paul Evans*

The year is 2010, and there is another September 29th that just arrived, and today makes 67 of them for us. Yes, another anniversary for us that we celebrated very quietly, just the two of us. The Lodi Musical Theater presented the play, South Pacific at Hutchins Street Square on Thursday, September 23rd - we attended the play and thought it was very good. Then on Friday afternoon we went to Applebee's for a nice dinner. Carol sent us a very nice azalea plant which we both appreciated. Some phone calls from the kids, and that just about did it for another year.

But I want this year to be the year where I finally tell my Mary how much she means to me in print. After Josh and Karen's beautiful wedding a week or so ago, I wonder if she feels cheated with the simple little wedding we had. Would she rather have made me wait until we had a little more time and money for a big wedding? After she found out what kind of a guy I truly was, would she really marry me? These are just a couple of things I ponder while I am trying to figure how to get 67 years on a couple of sheets of paper.

The kids gave us a nice 50th year celebration at St Luke's church with all our friends there. However on our 60th, we were going to Grace Church, and Bill and Carol both mortgaged their OUT HOUSES, and threw us a blast of a party with friends from both churches, and a lot of other people we knew. The other 65 anniversaries have come and gone without a lot excitement, but each one was important because it reminded us of the love we had shared through the previous year. Each year we search our hearts and say to each other, "I love you", and 67 "I love you's" makes a fair size pile.

The thing that is truly important is that the promise we made before God years ago, gets stronger every year. So now I am asking God to give me the words to print that will put my Mary on the pedestal of love and joy that she has shared with me over all these many years.

Where do we start?

Let's start at the place where I started this mess: late in the fall of 1941. It's the football season of my first year of college, and the biggest game of the year is on: Taft vs. Bakersfield; College and High School on the same night. Betty's boyfriend Marv is playing high school ball, and the only way she can go is for Dad to let us use the car. Since we have the car, and I am getting tired of going to football games alone, I decide to see if I can find a girl that would go with me. There is a girl that I knew from my high school days that I will just call El. I ask a girl from Belridge (who was a friend of El's) if she knew if El was dating anyone. She said that she didn't think so, but she knew she was writing to a soldier in the Army. I asked El if she would go to the football game with me and she said yes.

Betty and I hopped in Dad's car and headed for Taft where I picked up El, and then headed for Bakersfield. Marv was the high school quarter-back, and had called a perfect game so Taft won big time. The college game was a bit more of a struggle, but we won that game also. After the games we went to a drive-in, and yelled at all of the Bakersfield people about haw badly Taft beat them. We went back to Taft to drop off El, then to North Belridge to drop off Marv, and then Betty and I returned home to South Belridge. The following week, I asked El if she would like to take in a movie and a drive-in for a soda, and she agreed. After that we dated on and off for a few weeks, and finally found a place South of the City on a small hill by a old wooden derrick where we could do the things young couples do. We dated the rest of the school year, and did a lot of different things. We had several spats and disagreements, but usually before the night was over we were buddies again.

Near the end of the year I noticed her showing an 8x10 picture of her soldier to her friends in the college ladies lounge as I passed by. Were things more serious with them than I had thought? I really had this feeling that I was falling in love with El, but I wondered if I was just entertainment for her while she was waiting to see if her soldier was going to ask her to marry him.

About mid-summer I unexpectedly drove to Taft to see El, and as I drove up to the house she came out and told me she couldn't see me that night because she was going to a dance. I said, "OK El, I'll see you".

I felt destroyed. I thought we had a little something going.

After that I never, ever saw El again. She got a job working at a bank in town, and never returned to school. When I was in Navy Boot Camp, and was actively pursuing my Mary, I received letters from El and her mother on the same day. I answered the mother's letter, but all I got out of El's letter was that she had married the soldier.

I tore the letter up and burned it up with my cigarette lighter.

I didn't want it around anywhere. If she thought that I would answer that letter as hard as I was trying to convince my Mary how much I love her, she was surely mistaken.
The little bit that I do know about El, I learned from our high school class reunions. The first 10 year reunion she was listed with a last name different from her married name; it made me wonder if her first husband might have been killed in the war. The 20 year reunion had her listed as deceased - to bad she died so young.

I remained dateless until I started my second year of college. As a freshman, I had met a girl named Lela who had worked with me in Miss Pete's library. During my sophomore year I got up the courage to ask her out on a date. She was a high school senior that year and she agreed to go out with me. We had a few dates, and decided to go steady. She wore my letterman's sweater which told all the other guys to keep their hands off.

All went well until I innocently got in trouble when I was helping decorate a room for some college event with Margie, a girl that had been my friend all through high school and college.

Margie's mother had died several years before, leaving her dad with Margie, and two younger brothers to raise. They lived up on a hill above Taft about ten miles from the school. Her father was a friend of my uncle Bill's, and I had met her family at Huntington Lake one year when we were grade school age. While we were decorating the room, I asked Margie if she was going to come to the party that night. She said no because her father had to work and could not drive her to the school. Being such good friends for a long time, I asked Margie if she would come if I gave her a ride, and she said yes.

A couple of days later Lela was walking towards me with my sweater under her arm. She threw the sweater in my face and said, "Here's your sweater back." Lela had heard somewhere that what I did for Margie was some kind of romantic thing, instead of just helping a good friend get to the party.

So here I am back to square one: no girl friend with a tennis letter sweater that no one wants. Most girls want football letter sweaters; tennis letters are for sissies.

Now I tell you about these two girls to show you that I am not the greatest when it comes to hanging on to girl friends - a Romeo I am not.

But it was only a few months later when that little Ladybug I saw on the bus came into my life and stirred up my heart a little; maybe more than a little.

It was only about a month between the time I met my Mary, and our date to the college Mid-Winter Ball (I have written in a previous chapter how we spent this time mainly just being together as much as possible). During that month, I took Mary out to the refinery to meet my Uncle Bill one night. It was getting late, and I had to go back to Belridge to work the next day. I had pulled up in front of her house, and Mary hopped out and went out in front of the car to wave bye to me. I looked at her standing on the curb: cute little saddle shoes, bobby socks, dungarees, a pretty blouse, a big smile, and a lot of beautiful red hair; I turned the car off, got out and walked up to her, and made eye to eye contact. I put my arms around her, and then we made lip to lip contact.

Our first kiss and I think we both believed right then that we loved each other.

Standing there on the curb under the street light, before God and anyone else looking out the window, we kissed many, many more times before I could break away and go to Belridge. That little Ladybug found an open spot in my heart.

A couple of weeks later on the night of the Ball, I parked my father's car in front of Mary's house (Dads car was much nicer than mine, and this was a very special occasion), and knocked on the door. When it opened, there stood the most beautiful, most gorgeous person I had ever seen: a wonderful long formal, little white jacket, great smile, shining brown eyes, and beautiful red hair. She was no longer my little ladybug; she had become a young lady with the shining glory of one of God's Angels. I would never call her a ladybug again.

At the risk of repeating this story over and over, I will share one last thing. While driving Dad's car back to Belridge, I prayed this prayer, "God grant me the wisdom to be the person that I need be so that Mary will learn to love me as much as I love her." Statistically speaking, the odds of me keeping a girlfriend (a gambler would say), were stacked against me.

How did I get strayed so far from our 67th anniversary?

I think that it is very obvious that God answered my prayer. All these years Mary and I have shared Christ's love for each other. Mary and I have maintained two different habits in our lives when things are a little difficult. First, we don't go to sleep at night until unhappy feelings have been settled, and secondly, remember these two little words, "I'M SORRY".

It would be totally impossible for me to remember all of our anniversaries, but let me remember a few. The very first in1944: I am out somewhere in the pacific, wishing that I could be with Mary, and Mary is living with my parents. The second in 1945: still in the pacific, but in two months I would be discharged from the Navy. The third anniversary when both of us were living at home with our little Connie who was a month old. It is during this anniversary in Fresno where we suffered our first most devastating shock relating to Connie's birth and her brain damage. Doctors and friends encouraged us to put her into a hospital that cared for babies in that condition.

We decided against it.

For the next 14 years Mary dedicated her life to keeping Connie comfortable, healthy, and happy. Our carefree attitude changed, we were now the keepers of one of Gods little angels.

Just 4 months before our 12th anniversary, Carol, our second bundle from heaven, arrived – and that's when the whole family went to Hell (OK, this is Carol's MUCH younger brother adding his opinion on things while editing this chapter – Dad would never say anything like that about the "P", no matter how true it was). Very tiny and skinny, but in perfect health; praise God for that. About 3 months before our 16th anniversary, Bill our football player arrived (and things were much better at home then), also in perfect health; thank God again. Carol ate like a little bird, while Bill would eat everything in the house. Carol grew up to be about five feet tall, while Bill grew up to be six foot, three inches.

I have no anniversary dates for Sue and Mary - they just gradually melted their way into our hearts. For me they filled the void in my life that Connie had left when she passed away. I thank God for these precious little girls that made our family complete.

We celebrated our 65th anniversary trying to get over the loss of a buyer that backed out of the purchase we thought we had on our house in Fresno. However, the next year on our 66th anniversary, we celebrated with the sale of the Fresno home and moving to Lodi. With the great celebrations of our 50th and 60th, the above years are those that were significant to me as well. But in all honesty, all the others have been equally important to me.

I have come to believe that the anniversary celebration should be between a man, his wife, and God. First it is a celebration of the vow we made before God at our wedding. Second, it is a time to thank God for a chance to spend another year with your spouse. Third, it is a time to thank God for being allowed to raise his precious children that are still keeping their marriage vows. Fourth, the chance to pray to successfully reach number 71.

"If I could catch a rainbow I would do it just for you
And share with you its beauty
on days you're feeling blue.
If I could build a mountain you could call your very own,
A place to find serenity, a place to be alone.
If I could take your troubles I would toss them in the sea,
But all these things I'm finding are impossible for me.
I cannot build a mountain or catch a rainbow fair,
But let me be what I know best,
a husband who's always there."
- Author Unknown

Remember that uncle I captured to marry us?? He was a very successful Pentecostal Minister; he started and built a large church in Watsonville, California. Originally from Mississippi, he married my grandma's oldest daughter (the Grandma that was also a Pentecostal preacher). It was my Grandma that encouraged him to study for the ministry while he worked a job at the same time. I admired him very much, and was so happy that he was available for our wedding. Before he left he got me in a corner for some of that, "preacher stuff". The one thing I remember was when he told me, "Bud get your life right with Christ and you will be the head of a happy home, and have a great future."

All good advice, and I would do it; about 20 years down the road.

Chapter Nineteen

CHRISTMASES

"The little girl came into her Papa's study, as she always did Saturday morning before breakfast, and asked for a story. He tried to beg off that morning, for he was very busy, but she would not let him. "Well, once there was a little pig…" The little girl put her hand over his mouth and stopped him at that word. She said she had heard the pig stories till she was perfectly sick of them. Well what kind of a story shall I tell then? About Christmas; it's getting to be the season, it's past Thanksgiving already. It seems, argued her Papa, I've told as often about Christmas as I have about little pigs.

No difference! But Christmas is more interesting."
- Richard Paul Evans

I'm grateful for the Christmases of my life

I think the little girl was right; Thanksgiving is still to come, and the stores are moving in Christmas things already. Can't they wait and let us celebrate one holiday at a time? They take the meaning out of a beautiful Thanksgiving dinner. Winter will come soon enough, and when it comes we're going to ask ourselves, "Where did the years go?" It's winter before you know it. Our life span as one winter is long for some, while short for others. In June of 1941, Taft High School graduated a large senior class. Probably 80% of the men in that group went off to war. Of which over half had their winter over very soon as they never returned home. For some like me, we had lifelong winters. Many of us are just waiting for that last Christmas and for our winter to come to an end.

I remember only one Christmas at sea while my winter was passing. I was at the invasion of the Gilbert Islands. The Marines had invaded Tarawa, with the winter ending for 3700 marines who died there. After the island was secure, we spent most of December back at Makin Island (a known Japanese Submarine base) where we performed submarine patrols to intercept any returning Japanese subs that weren't aware that the US had taken the island back. We celebrated that Christmas season with a sign saying, "MAKING MERRY AT MAKIN". December 25, 1943, we sailed back to Pearl for pre-invasion training for the Marshall Islands.

Back in the days in 1935, when we moved in at Belridge, money was kind of on the scarce side. I know my father had lots of bills to pay, and though I don't really remember, I would think that our Christmases were very skimpy. I'm sure that there was a gift or two for each of us. Our parents would have made sure of that. As the years rolled by and the bills got paid, the gifts got larger. I remember one year I got my first bicycle and that was a long awaited gift for me.

The Christmases I remember most were those after the war was over, and we had started raising our families. Betty and Marv lived in San Diego with their daughter Sharon, Mary and I and our little Connie were in Fresno, and Lois was still a teenager living at home. All off us met that first year at the folks place in Belridge. It was more than a Christmas celebration; it was the first time we had all been together after the war. As the years passed it seemed there was another grandchild to bless

our Christmas. Gary was Betty and Marv's second child.
About this time, Lois and Bob met and were married,
which completed the adults in the family.

Our Carol, and Bob and Lois's Mary, were both very
close in age and the next grandchildren. Probably about
four years later, our son Bill, and Lois and Bob's George,
both also very close in age, were added to the family. A
couple years later, the last blessing we received was
Lois and Bob's little Sabrina. The time had come for
God to put the zipper on children, he seemed to say,
"Let some other people have some of these little
children."

For many years our family was blessed and we were all
able to load up "the old station wagon" with gifts and
kids, and head for grandmother's and grandfather's
house for a wonderful Christmas.

I remember one year Betty and Marv gave Gary an
electric train and an erector set for Christmas. Neither
Marv nor I had ever received an erector set or electric
train for Christmas so we were very busy all that day
building bridges for the train to go over, and all kinds of
buildings.

One of our greatest fun things was to play Santa Claus
for the grandkids; Belridge had an old Santa suit that
they would let us use. Marv and I would take turns
playing Santa for the kiddos. One year it was Marv's
turn and all the children were out of the room where (he)
Santa was setting out gifts for the kids. Unexpectedly
the kids walked in and caught Santa in their own house.
Marv was setting up a toy ironing board for little Mary
when she quickly grabbed on to Georgie, walked him

right up to Santa and said, "Santa this is my little brother Georgie, and he needs a gift too."

One year when it was my turn to play Santa, Betty's little Sharon was beginning to question the truth about Santa. I had all the gifts out when the kids all showed up and got their gifts. After it was all over, Sharon went up to her mother and said. "That wasn't Santa, that was Uncle Bill."

Sort of blew my gift of being Santa after that.

Betty and I would spend the whole year trying to think up some kind of nasty little gifts for each other. Some times they bordered the edge for little eyes though. We had to watch that and remember we had a house full of God's little children. Lois always said that before she was married, she would never bring a boyfriend to our Christmas Eve party because she would have to explain the gifts that Betty and I exchanged.

These are the memories that I love; the memories of yesteryear. These children of yesteryear are now the parents, and in some cases the grandparents; and that is how God intended it to be.

"For this reason a man shall leave his father and mother, and be united to his wife, and the two will become one flesh." Ephesians 5:31.

The grandparents of yesteryear are long gone; and even Betty's Marv, my Santa Clause brother, is now gone.

Lois and Bob, Betty, and Mary and I are in the late years of grand-parenting. I know for a fact that all of yesteryear's children have kept Gods teaching and have themselves mostly grown children. Our own children each have their own little family Christmas, and than a family Christmas for those who can gather at someone's home. I have seen some beautiful Christmases at both Bill and Carol homes.

Christmas with Bill and Cathy

Christmas in Fresno and Belridge are not the Christmases I have shared with the kids. I remember well the first Christmas we shared with Bill and Cathy in their new house in Reno Nevada along with Tim, Carol, and little Tommy. Snow on the ground, hoarfrost hanging in the trees, and ice everywhere. "Watch out for that ice Dad" when they saw me sitting on my butt. Nice warm home, fire in the fireplace, Christmas tree in the corner, and some good smells coming from the kitchen.

Cozy....cozy-----cozy-----cozy.

BUT on Christmas day in Reno there is a game of golf!!! There was a 9 hole golf course down on the edge of Reno; so bundle up little 2 year old Tommy, and lets go celebrate Christmas. NOW, what we didn't know was that the golf course is the favorite winter spot for a group of Canadian Honkers. I am sure you know what those big old honkers do just eating and dropping leavings all over the course. Because of the leavings, our little Tommy grew 2 inches with it stuck on his little boots. I guess I would say that I would give a two thumbs up for a Christmas Mary and I had never seen.

Also the Christmas we shared with Tim and Carol in their condo was exciting. It was late Friday night, two car loads of people floated into the town of Newport Oregon. True to what most believe, it started to rain at the California - Oregon border, and rained all the way to our destination. The lead car had Bill, Mom, and I, and the second was Cathy with all four boys. Mom and I were dropped off at Tim and Carol's ocean-side condo to stay with them, while Bill and Cathy had a Time Share about ten miles a way.

Mom and I had been to the condo several times, so we knew what a beautiful place it was already. It sets high on a mountainside overlooking the beach and ocean as far north as you can see. To the south you can see the Yaquina Head Lighthouse. It is a very wonderful place with 2 bedrooms, 2 baths, nice size kitchen and living room. The next morning Mom and I went into Newport with Carol to get a little Christmas tree, and decorated it with decorations Carol had brought from home. About noon the other group showed up in time for lunch. After lunch, people just scattered: some went shopping, some went down on the beach to build sand castles, some played golf, and some just flopped down for a nap.

Our seven grandsons were the happiest when they could all be together, and this was one of those times. We had our gifts that night, Christmas Eve. The next day Carol prepared a great dinner for all of us, and then just like the day before, everyone scattered. The weather had been cold and icy, but no snow. Sadly the day after Christmas was Monday, and we all scattered for home; the fun time was over for another year.

Another two thumbs up for Tim and Carol's Christmas too.

I remember another cold, cold, cold Christmas. It was another one at Bill and Cathy's in their new home in Bend, Oregon. It was even too cold for golf that year. I took a big box of California oranges up that year, and set them in the garage that night thinking they would be safe in there. WRONG; the next morning all I had was a box full of orange stones. It got so cold that year that it cracked the pick-up canopy in several places - the company I bought it from replaced it for free.

Now I will be the first to admit that I hate the cold weather with a passion, but I will be the first to admit that a city with about 8 inches of snow on the ground at Christmas time is beautiful. A few years ago the same group that attacked Tim and Carol's condo attacked them again at their home in Salem. Leaving Lodi for Oregon at Christmas, the biggest concern is, "Do the Siskiyou Mountains have enough snow that we have to chain up the cars to get over them?" The year we went to the condo we got only as far as Redding where the highway was closed, and we had to spend the night there. However this trip the highway was open, rain but no snow; and no chains - all the way to Salem.

However, the Commercial Street exit comes off of Interstate Drive, drops down under the freeway and goes West into town - at this point the ground had 6 inches of snow as far as the eye can see - snow everywhere. We stopped at our mobile home and put out the dogs (Tim had turned on the furnace, so the house was nice and warm), and then we headed for Carol and Tim's. We had to park at the top of the hill because with all that snow, we thought we would never get out of his driveway if we drove down to their house. Tim taxied us back and forth from our house to theirs with his 4-wheel drive pick-up. Christmas went on like it did at the condo - lots of shoppers, but no golfers this year. I have to say the most beautiful thing of the season was the snow constantly falling the entire time we were there.

I had heard of Christmases like this, and read of Christmases like this, but this was the first time I ever experienced anything so beautiful. The kids did everything they could to make it a great Christmas, but I think we must say that this one was a God given one:

He provided the snow.

Good-Bye Ol' Friend

Mary and I were standing out in the cold looking at our little mobile home with about 8 inches of snow on the roof. We had never seen it with so much snow, and Mary said, "I'm glad that old cedar tree is long gone, I bet it would have lost some limbs with all this snow."

Yes, the old cedar tree - that's a story that needs to be

told and now is a good time to do it.

When we bought the mobile home it had a great big cedar tree growing very close to our house. It was a bit of a nuisance with its small cones that fell, and leaves that had to be raked up - but I put up with it. A time or two, a fair sized limb had fallen on the house. It did no damage, but we were a little concerned about it when the wind blew real hard. Some years later I noticed that the tree roots were raising the concrete slab that my front deck sat on, and was causing my exterior paneling to crinkle up.

It was time to do something about it.

It was the beginning of October, and in about two weeks we would head south for the winter. As luck would have it, I was out side when the owner of the park sauntered by. She said good morning, and I immediately called her attention to the tree problem. She asked, "What do you want me to do about it?" I said, "Take the tree down." She said, "Humph", and walked away like that was the most ridiculous thing she had ever heard.

The challenge was on. I went into the house, got out my little typewriter, and sat down to plead my case. I wrote, "In regard to the tree that we talked about, and you so rudely walked away, this is to inform you that we will be going home to Fresno in two weeks for the winter. While we are there I will seek out legal advice, and we will continue the conversation about removing the tree next May. I can not allow the tree to damage my house."

I sent it by registered mail, and two days later the owner informed me that the tree would come down. The next week on Monday morning the tree remover was all set to take down the tree and the park exploded. I found out that everyone in the park thought it was the most beautiful tree because it was the first thing they saw when they entered the park. There was so much complaining that the manager of the park stopped the tree man because the owner of the park was away for the day, and he wanted to consult with her first. The next day the owner advised me that the tree would come down regardless of what the people said.

Now I will be the first to admit that it was a beautiful tree but what was I to do? I'll tell you what we did: the next day when the tree man was to return to cut down the tree, we hopped in the car before daylight and headed to Fresno for the Winter - and LET THE CHIPS FALL WHERE THEY MAY.

Well I could go on and on about Christmases, it seems to me that it is always the last one that we think was the best. Scriptures are very important in their judgment into the number of Christmases we can expect to have to celebrate. In Psalms 90:10, a prayer of Moses says, "The length of our days is seventy years--or eighty, if we have the strength; yet their span is trouble and sorrow, for they quickly pass, and we fly away."

Now as I understand that scripture, it would seem to me that I am entitled to as many Christmases as years. Since I am now ninety-one, eleven years beyond the eighty God promised me, there might not be a great lot of Christmases in my future. I will take them one day at a time, and I promise to be happy wherever they are held. I would hope to fellowship with as many of my family as possible, share my love with each of them, and

I will be very thankful to God for each Christmas I have left.

Tim and Carol's First Snowy House

A little humor:

THE FOUR STAGES OF LIFE

1) You believe in Santa Claus
2) You don't believe in Santa Claus
3) You are Santa Claus
4) You look like Santa Claus

Chapter Twenty

THE RETIREMENT

*"My announcement was about as well received as
a bowl of soup with a hair in it."*

*"So often the pain in our lives is no more than a
reminder to take our hand off the stove."*
-Richard Paul Evans

*"Happy days are here at last. The days of 9 to 5 are
past. I've worked all my life and paid my dues, now I'll
do just what I choose!"*

*"Retirement is a time when you never get around to
doing all those things you intended to do when you were
still working."*

*"When one door closes, another opens, but we often
look so long and regretfully at the closed door we fail to
see the one that has opened for us."*

*"When I die, I want to go peacefully like my grandfather
did - in his sleep.
Not yelling and screaming like the passengers in his
car."*

*"God, grant me the senility to forget the people I never
liked anyway, the good fortune to run into the ones I do,
and the eyesight to see the difference."*

Is there any doubt what this chapter is going to cover? If
there is let me explain:

RETIREMENT!!!!

I hired on with P.G.&E. November 14, 1945, and left February 14, 1982: 36 years, 6 months.

I started at P.G.&E. as a Rodman, Probationary; Pay rate $6.36 per day. On November 21, 1945 I became a Transit Man B, Probationary (Recommended above starting wage due to past experience and qualifications). I was employed as a Transit man due to the increase in work; Pay Rate $8.40 per day.

I had just finished a week in the blue print room trimming maps when about noon, Glen walked into the blue print room and said, "Bill, did you learn enough about trimming maps to run a survey crew? I need a crew to survey 14 miles of telephone line Monday morning, and your it." Glen hired two U.S. Air Force Captains who had just been recently discharged as my crew. One, Travis, had been a Navigator. The other, Bob, was a Glider Pilot; both knew less about surveying than I did. I think about the words of our Lord "The blind leading the blind." Well it took us about a week to stumble and fumble our way through the 14 miles with one major problem - a part of the telephone line went right through a corral that held a big White Faced Bull with a ring in his nose - the whole bit; and he was on guard of his pen.

Neither of my brave captains would accept the challenge to drag the chain through the corral. They would ride a bomber through the air over Germany, or take their chances in a Glider, but no way would either of them go into that pen with that Bull. Soooo what do you do: a good boss never asks his men to do something he wouldn't do. I grabbed the end of the chain and shoved it through the fence slowly, then climbed the fence, cautiously (but very quickly I might add) drug the chain to the other side of the pen, climbed the fence on the other side of the pen, and then got out.

Job well done.

I turned my notebook into the Draftsman who immediately started pulling at his hair (which he had very little of to start with). He said, "These are the worst notes I ever saw." He then showed me what I should do, and what I should not do. I said, "Don I'm here for the long haul. So don't give up on me." The three of us worked together for several months. Travis worked for the company before he went into the service so he requested a job that was offered in the Gas Meter Department and got it. Bob on the other hand told Glen that I worked him to hard so he just up and quit. Without a crew, that might have been my first thoughts about retirement.

> "May you always have work for your hands to do.
> May your pockets always hold a coin or two.
> May the sun shine bright on your windowpane.
> May a rainbow be certain to follow the rain.
> May the hand of a friend always be near you.
> And may God fill your heart with gladness to cheer you."

I have no idea when it started, but shortly after I started work, P.G.& E. came out with a stock plan for the employees. For every $1.00 the employee put into the plan, the company would put in another $0.50. The amount the employee could invest was a certain percentage of his monthly wage. My big boss at that time told us when he introduced the program, "If you guys take advantage of this, you could come out with over a $100,000 when you retire."

My thought was it would be good for the children's education, if not for future retirement. I contributed the maximum amount that I could, and saved it in it's entirety for all the years I worked. Fortunately we did not have to use any of it for education, and had the entire amount to use for retirement. In the middle of 1980, an agent from Morgan Stanley explained the procedure to follow going into retirement. At the age of 59 years, 6 months, we could take our share out and put it in a joint account. There were no taxes due on that account. The company's share would go into an I.R A. account, and taxes would be paid according to the plan's procedure. We were able to draw the dividends from both accounts to supplement our retirement. The 2,666 shares in my account, and 1,333 shares in the company's account would be a big help with our future income. At 59 ½, that meant the soonest I could possibly retire was February 14, 1982. If I worked beyond that time, I would get more in my retirement pay, and my Social Security income would be a little higher. What to do?

I tell myself it's time to spend some quality time up on the rock at triangulation point "C", which I did many times over the next two years.

I spent time with friends who retired early, and time with friends who worked to 65 years of age. I spent time with our pastor, and people who had a strong Christian walk. I talked and prayed with Mary, trying to do what was best for our family. The surveying field was changing rapidly with new electronic equipment replacing the labor of dragging a chain all over the field. I heard surveyors say they could lay out an entire subdivision with these new transits setting up from one spot, with the assistance of only rodman, and Computers were beginning to come into some of the offices.

Maybe I should get out instead of having to learn a new kind of surveying.

At this point we were well into 1981; if I am going to retire in February of 1982, I needed to start making arrangements to let it be known. I got my survey crews all ready to go out into the field for the days work. I pick up a few jobs that my crews will do, and headed for North Fork to my famous old Triangulation Point "C". I knelt down on the big old rock and started to pray. I don't know how long I talked to God - time was not important, but before I left that day I had a peace of mind that I should go ahead with the early retirement. The next morning I went into the Personal Department to notify them of my decision, and then told my Boss, and everyone in the office including my survey crews.

Everyone was shocked because none of them had any idea that I was even considering retirement. Many people tried to get me to change my mind, but I told them I was confident with my decision. They threw me a big retirement party with friends coming from all over Northern California and the San Joaquin Valley: Sacramento, San Francisco, and from Merced South to Bakersfield. The company had a special dinner for me, and it was a wonderful send off.

After 37 years it was a change for me to get up in the morning watch the rest of the family get up and head off for work: Bill and Cathy off to some hospital somewhere, and Mary off to her school job that she loved so dearly. I stood there in the kitchen with a cup of coffee in my hand and watched the two dogs go through the doggie door headed for the back yard leaving me all alone wondering what happened so fast. I didn't realize how quickly everyone disappeared in the morning. The T. V. was silent, the coffee pot was empty, and I don't know how to make any more. One good thing though, the bathroom is empty and that's a first for me. I can go in any time I want to now with no one banging on the door.

Soooooooo this is what retirement is all about.

Maybe I'll get dressed and go down to the Old Coffee Shop and see if any of the old gang is there. No, they must be at another shop. By now the golfers have already teed off, and were halfway around the course. I guess its back to the house for me. What was all those things I was going to do around the house when I retired? Mow the lawn? That's it, but this is Monday and I already mowed it Saturday - that won't work. Was there something about painting the bathroom? No, it's the middle of February and that's to close to winter - not supposed to paint in the winter time. What about that ugly drippy shower and bath tub water faucet, it needs to be replaced? Where to start? The Hardware Store of course. Keep it simple remember just like the one you take out.

I studied the tile on the wall around the faucet and realized that the wall on the other side was in the hall way. I could open up a hole on that side and didn't have to disturb the tile. I gathered up all the tools I still had from the work on the cabin, got everything I needed from the Hardware Store, and told everyone to take a shower that would last for three days because I was going to start the next day. I opened up the wall and saw that everything was as I suspected it would be, turned off the water, and got the show on the road. I replaced the faucet - no water leaks - then put plaster back over the hole, stuck a piece of furniture in front of the evidence, and once again the shower was working. For a couple of days, people got a little stinky, but after a shower all was forgiven.

Mom handed me anther project for me to consider: How about WE wallpaper the bathroom? She handed me the paper she had decided on, and said lots of luck, I'll see you tonight. "Anyone can put paper on the wall. I'll be done by noon, and can play golf this afternoon." NOT SO. It took me all that day and two more to finish the job. It was even more of a challenge when about a month later the steam from the shower made some of the paper peel loose.

Next, Mom said, "While you still have wall paper cement in your hair, how about WE wallpaper the kitchen also." After the bathroom chore, I allowed a full week for the kitchen because there was also a lot of painting to do. "Wow, I didn't know you were such a good painter. Why don't WE paint the living room and dining room too?" Mom said.

She's never going to let me back on the golf course again. Never, ever again.

This little project included the entry way, hall-way, and the walls up the stair-way. With my paint roller the walls were a piece of cake, but painting the trim around the doors, windows, and the floor took forever. My Mary, with her eagle eye, thought it looked so nice that she let me do the two down stairs bedrooms too.

My lucky day!!

After WE got all of the inside work done to everyone's approval, then we had new carpeting put down throughout the house down stairs. I didn't think I had worked 37 years so my house could look like it did, but I was very proud of the way everything turned out.

One of the projects I had put off until retirement was to put a sprinkler system in both the front and back yards. I had some problems with the main water line from the street to my house, so the first thing to do was to get a plumber to replace that line for me. At the same time I had him put a line under the house to hook up the back yard sprinklers. I figured I could use about 8 rain bird sprinklers in the backyard so I started digging trenches. Once I had the trenches dug, I truly enjoyed working with the PVC Pipe and Fittings. This job allowed me time for golf, an occasional visit at lunch with a friend from work, and time off when the weather was to hot to work in.

The front yard was a little more of a challenge though because it was cut up into three sections, so I had to use smaller but more numerous sprinklers. That meant more trenches. One Sunday morning after I had most of my trenches dug I received a phone call that my mother had passed away, so everything came to a halt for several weeks. Finally I got the job finished and hooked up all the wiring. After a few adjustments, I said to myself, "Good job - go play golf."

Mary worked about a year and a half after I did and then she retired. Now we could do things together. We had things to do and places to go. We were REALLY retired, and summer was almost here; it was almost time to head for Oregon. This year we could stay until October if we chose to.

This is retirement!!!!!!!!!

It's time to dance again Babe

Goodbye to work, you are on high
You don't have to ask why!
You now gladly say adieu to your working life
Goodbye to toil and strife.
Tomorrow, when morning comes at noon,
You will lie in bed and look up at the ceiling.
There will be no one there to give orders or more work
What a great feeling.
As the noon sun shines through your window,
You will hear a dog bark and the noise of someone's feet.
It's the letter carrier, poor working soul,
Delivering your mail, you can hear him in the street.
Within you will come a warning glow
Your new life will have just begun.
This is the day that you have looked forward to
Knowing that all your work has been done.
Shortly you will arise, get dressed, and relax
There's still time left in the day for much merry-making.
You will make the most of it knowing that most of your friends

Are at work, stressed, and mentally aching.
Will there be any reason to feel any
Stress of guilt at this time of your life?
Only when you forget to wake up early
And make breakfast for your poor working wife.
- Dave Erhard

Next February I will start my 32nd year of retirement. Do I have any regrets for taking an early retirement? I think that in the story of my life, having big bucks is quite far down on the list of what is important. What was important was driving the back roads of Oregon, with a stop at an inn for lunch, watching Tommy, Teddy, and Josh grow up, and tons of fun things. Would I retire early again?

IN A MINUTE.

I think that at this time I must go back to a statement I made earlier in the book. That being, "Mary and I decided against my going back to school. Instead get out and get a job first." or something to that effect. I think that what I saw in my father in the depression years had more of an influence on me as a boy than I ever thought. The dream of him trying to find work during those years remained with me all my life. My father worked for Belridge for 35 years, just as I worked for P.G.&E for 37 years. I never wanted to change my job, and try something that might have been better. I'm a "hanger-on", a "keeper"; I like what I got: security.

Let me leave you with a little story of a Keeper I knew: Their marriage was good, their dreams focused. Their best friends lived barely a wave away. I can see them now, Dad in his trousers, tee shirt and hat, working on the lawn mower, and Mom in her house dress, dish-towel in her hand. It was a time for fixing things. A curtain rod, the kitchen radio, screen door, the oven door, the hem in a dress. Things we keep. It's was a way of life and sometimes it made me crazy. All that re-fixing, eating, and renewing - I wanted just once to be wasteful. Waste meant affluence. Throwing things away meant you knew there'd always be more. But then mother died, and on that clear summer's night, in the warmth of the hospital room, I was struck with the pain of learning that sometimes there isn't any more. Sometimes, what we care about most gets all used up and goes away never to return. So while we have it, it's best to love it, fix it when it's broken, and heal it when it's sick. This is true for marriages, old cars, children with bad report cards, dogs and cats with bad hips, aging parents, and grandparents. We keep them because they are worth it, like people we know who are special. And so we keep them close, like my father and my mother: they were KEEPERS.

I know that I am sometimes forgetful. But there again, some of life is just as well forgotten, but I'll eventually remember the important things. So don't mess with the old man hobbling down the sidewalk leaning over his cane. Remember that seniors didn't get there by being stupid.

Chapter Twenty-One

NEW HOME AND OLD WHEELS

*"Is this life, to grasp joy only to fear its escape?
The price of happiness is to risk losing it."*

*"Summer is a fever of sorts, hot and deceptive,
like falling in love."*
- Richard Paul Evans

It's the summer of 1986; we were sitting in our trailer that was set up in Salem at a mobile home park. Tim and Carol live all the way across town, and we are wondering if we could find a place closer to their house. We found a mobile home park on Sunnyside Road that would be less than a mile from them, and decided to go and check it out. A very nice park; we drive through and see nothing that looks like a travel trailer space, so we stop and talk to a very friendly manager and his wife. They told us that they did not have any spaces for our trailer but, would we be interested in buying a mobile home? He said he had a place for sale that we could look at.

The house was on the far East side of the park, and was at the bottom of a bluff that had a row of houses on top. It was a very nice two bedroom, two bath mobile home that was in nice condition, but we decided it wasn't something we were excited about. The location with the houses looking down on the home for one thing, and we would not feel comfortable leaving it through the winter in that spot.

When we got back to the office, the wife said that the house on the corner across the street was going to be for sale in about a month. She told her husband to go see if the lady would show it. The owner answered yes so we got a look. She said that she wanted to take a trip to the Black Forrest in Germany, and it would be a month before she could sell the place; she told us she would be asking $17,000 for the home. That evening we brought Tim and Carol to look at the place, and the four of us talked long into the night about it.

"When one door closes, another one opens, but we often look so long and regretfully at the closed one, that we fail to see the one that has been opened to us."
- Alexander Graham Bell
-

Our Heavenly Home

After much prayer, the next day Mary and I went out to see the lady to tell her she had a deal. She gave us a date that she would be back from Germany, and we could complete the deal then. I asked her if she wanted some money down, and she said, "Let's just shake hands on it." So that is just what we did.

True to her word, at the end of the month we met, and she had in her mind just how we would change ownership. First we went to the Tax Collector's Office and paid our portion of the taxes, then to the Department of Motor Vehicles, followed with a trip to the Insurance Office, then we shook hands again and the house was ours. She asked if we would allow her a week to move; we said yes and then left immediately for Fresno to get a load of furniture. We had living room furniture from my mother's house that I loaded into our suburban and headed back to Salem, and we bought a bedroom set from the lady when we made the deal. From J. C. Penney's we bought a small dining room table with four chairs. Then we headed for Mervyns and bought the kitchen things we needed.

The Park had a storage space for our travel trailer, so we went over to the other park, hooked up the trailer, and brought it to our new home to put it in storage. Some people have cabins in the mountains, some people have condos on the coast, some people have timeshares all over the country; we had a cottage in a bit of heaven, where we spent the summers for the next twenty-four years.

The house just had a set of steps in front that sat on an 8x10 foot concrete pad which I wanted to do something about. The next trip to Fresno I brought back all the tools I had from working on the cabin those many years ago. I went to the lumber yard with mega bucks in both pockets and bought enough cedar 2x4 and 2x6 to build a nice 8x10 foot deck about 2 foot high, with a railing all around it. Everyone in the park had to walk past our house when they went to the office to pick-up their mail. Don't you know that I got a lot of very special advice on what I was doing. When I finished I also replaced the back steps with matching cedar like the front, and gave them both a good coat of outdoor cedar stain.

Here's our new patio

The southwest corner of my lot had another 8x12 foot concrete pad. About a year after we moved in I built a 6x8 foot covered area on the end, and put an 8 foot picnic table under it. Now we had a nice patio area for our three grandsons. This kind of upset some of the neighbors, but I got permission from the owner to build it.

A year after that, I discover that if I move the 24 foot metal awning and shed of my carport 8 feet towards the street, I will have another 8x9 foot concrete pad, and room to put a small building. The owner, being happy with the building that I have already done, agrees to let me go to work. The metal awning and shed, being anchored into the concrete, was a bit of a challenge, but I got it loose. I put rollers under the shed, picked up the awning posts and moved it 8 feet, then anchored it all back into the concrete. A few more trips back to the lumber yard and I built an 8x9 foot building with wood paneling on the outside, one window, and a door all painted to match the house. Then I put a sign on the door that said, "JIM'S PLACE." I hung wood paneling on the inside walls, acoustic tile on the ceiling, lights, a ceiling fan, and a T. V. antenna outside. I put a big table under the window, and hung all my hand tools on the wall. Then I went to Fresno and brought back all of my stained glass tools, along with a small T.V.. I'm in business again, and being in Oregon made it a much cooler place then Fresno.

Life in a Senior Mobile Home park was a completely strange thing for me; lots and lots of people. There is the one who has been in the park ever since it has been built, and who knows the history of everyone in the park, including the manager and his wife. She is the one who meets you as soon as you unlock your front door with a dish of cookies in one hand, and a couple of marigolds in the other, clacking her false teeth as she talks. In just a quick two-hour visit, she will enlighten you about who you are supposed to like, those you are to hate, those you are to avoid, and those you are to watch; especially the two guys in B-2 - they are a little bit strange. Why did we pick this park because the rent is the highest in the state? Are you or your kids using dope or weed, and what day do you take your bath; the water pressure is better on Wednesday. Watch the guy two doors down from you, and the guy across the street, they are both golfers and they cheat and steal.

Well everything she said was true except that the two guys she mentioned were the best golfing friends I ever had; however they did cheat at times. I got hooked on golf a long time before we bought the mobile home. It was one day when Sue and Randy were down from Washington visiting Tim and Carol. It was a beautiful afternoon, and Randy and Tim decided to go golfing, and they asked me to go with them. No way, I had never had a golf club in my hand, and had no intention to start now. If they wanted to play a few sets of tennis, I was good for that. "You guys go ahead without me", I said. Not good enough for them, I had to go. I rented a bag of clubs, and went eighteen holes with the boys – I was HOOKED.

I went back to Fresno and bought a set of golf clubs. I discovered that Leonard, pastor of Mary's parent's Nazarene church, along with two other Nazarene pastors, played golf every Monday, and invited me to join them. Other men from their churches joined the group, and I played with these new friends for many years. Even when we got the mobile home and were gone all summer, they were still there when I returned to Fresno in the winter.

Now back to the new mobile home. The guy two doors down turned out to be Eddie. Eddie was a U.S. Navy veteran of World War II. He was on three destroyers that had been sunk, and he survived each one; but had lost half his right foot from the last one. You have heard the old saying, "cuss like a sailor"? I think that Eddie invented that saying because he could cuss a blue streak. At least 75% of the words out of his mouth were cuss words. Eddie was also a coffee drinker; he always had two pots going, one in his house and one in his shop. He had a cup in his hand all the time. He and his lovely wife loved to travel in their RV; but more than that, Eddie loved to play golf. With a couple of thermos bottles of coffee in his golf bag and he was good for the day.

The guy across the street was Don. Don was also a U.S. Navy veteran Seabee, in both World War II and the Vietnam War. Don could do his share of cussing, but he was not as proficient as was Eddie. Don was also a golfer; in fact, he might have been a little better than Eddie and me. However, neither of us would admit it because a kick of the ball (for a better lie), or forgotten stroke kept the scores fairly close. There were several golf courses in the neighborhood, so there was a good chance that a game was in the making if two of us were together; if three of us were together it was be a sure thing. Occasionally Don's brother-in-law, Les from Utah, came over for a couple of weeks making a foursome, and we enjoyed playing with him.

This was great fun for several years until the park owner raised the rent a sizable amount. Eddie said, "I would not pay that @#%$&*&^%#$# much rent. I'll sell this @#^%$*&#@@@ house and move out". And *&^%$#@%$#&&* is what he did. He bought another mobile home on about a half acre piece of property in Lebanon, which was about 18 miles south of Salem. For many years the three of us would meet in Albany (about equidistant from Lebanon and Salem) once or twice a week at a golf course, until Eddies wife Rosetta's health got so bad that he could no longer leave her to play with us. So Don and I stopped playing in Albany, and just played around Salem. The last I heard of Eddie, both he and his wife were in a 24 hour care facility. Don's wife,

Irene, died and he was alone for about five years. Then he moved to Washington State to live with his son. About four years ago Les phoned me that Don had passed away. Just Les and I are all that's left, and neither of us play any more.

Many of the people we met at the mobile home park became close friends. Don and Irene, Eddie and Rosetta, Frank and Doris, Vick and Doris, Chris, Kenny and Imogene, Bob and Emma – but alas most of these dear friends are long gone. You also had some just casual acquaintances that you only said "Hi" to, and others that you just ignored. Probably one of our greatest thrills was my sister Lois and her husband Bob stopping at our little place after their tour of the northwest. We had such a great time when we took them on a day trip to Lincoln City on the Oregon coast. Another of the great things in the park was that we had our travel trailer right there in a storage space, so it was ready for a quick little trip to a coast campground.

One day we got a letter from Betty that they were going to travel in their camper to Brookings, Oregon to visit Marv's brother Norman and wife Ruth, and they wanted to know if we could meet them there. We threw a few spuds in the trailer and off we went. After a few days visiting, we traveled north on the Oregon coast to Florence, where we spent the night at Jessie Honeyman State Park. The next day we continued up the coast to Astoria where we spent another night at the Fort Stevens State Park. The next morning we crossed the Columbia River on a huge long bridge leading to the Washington side. We then drove south on the east side of the river to Hood River, and then crossed the river back again to the Oregon side to take a ride on the Stern

Wheeler (a riverboat steamer). Then we followed the Columbia River back to Portland, and then turned south all the way to Lodi for a visit with Lois and Bob. After that we headed home to Fresno, while Marv and Betty continued on to San Diego.

Two different times Tim led us to the far northeast corner of Oregon to Wallowa Lake State Park; six miles out of the town of Joseph. The park is on the south end of a beautiful lake. The lake is important because it was the first time that our Teddy caught about a 14 inch rainbow trout. He was upset because Tim told him he couldn't mount it and we had to eat it. Tears flowed, but I think he thought it was also very good eating. As I recall we spent a week there, and the park was full of huge beautiful deer with huge racks of horns. They would stand with their forefeet on the step of the trailer and peek in the door looking for food.

On our way back to Salem, we spent one more night in another state park. As we pulled in, the Ranger cautioned us that a bear had been into the garbage cans the night before. He told us to be very alert, and careful with our foods. He said if the bear came back and was a problem, they would have to shoot him. We had a nice evening with a nice camp fire, and then went to bed. To get an early start and miss the heat, we got up about 6:00 am. Tim started his Jeep Wagoner, and when he did it let out a big loud explosion. People from all over the camp came running out of their tents and trailers yelling, "THEY SHOT THE BEAR". When they discovered it wasn't true, everyone huddled around with advice on how to fix the jeep. A year or two later, we would repeat this beautiful trip with Sue and Randy and their kids. I forgot to mention that there was a nice little nine hole golf course in Joseph. We three big boys got to play there a couple of times.

Another great stop we all enjoyed was a trailer park just north of the Yaquina Head Lookout in Newport, Oregon. Tim and Carol had their motor home then, and Randy and Sue would use Randy's parent's motor home. Our trailer was always open for early coffee, chocolate, and a newspaper before breakfast.

Twice we went to Yellowstone National Park - one of the times with Randy, Sue, and their kids. On that trip we ended up in Glacier National Park along the Canadian Boarder and we played golf there as well. We had some great times with our children while living in our mobile home.

I had towed my trailer with a Chevrolet Suburban Truck, which I loved very much. It had a very large motor in it (I think it was a 454, whatever that was). It was a good backing truck: I could back my trailer into most places without a lot of effort. Only one time did it let me down; we were following Tim, Carol, and their boys in their RV up along a steep grade. We were on our way home by way of Sue and Randy's place, from our first Yellowstone trip. All of a sudden, POW and oil started spraying everywhere. I had broken one of the oil lines to my transmission cooler. Tim came back and saw what had happened, then drove on to a small town ahead. He got the parts needed to fix us up, and we were soon on the road.

It had to be about 1970, or there about, that my folks bought a Chevrolet pick-up with a nice new camper on it, and they decided to take a trip back to Missouri (where mother was born) and see if they could find her birth place. They viewed the Grand Canyon, Dads birth place in the mining town of Jerome, Arizona, and many other beautiful places on their way. My sister Betty ended up with Mother's daily log book of their trip years before. Betty, Marv, Mary, and I thought it would be fun to take the book our Mother had written and retrace their trip. We loaded up our trailer, and they loaded their camper, and we met in Barstow, California at the place the folks had started their trip.

We got to see Jerome, then on to the town of Follett, Texas which was the home of Marv's mother's relatives, aunts uncles cousins; just a bunch of real nice people. They made Marv a nice deal, if he would come back again on his way home, they would have big family reunion. We went on with the trip stopping in the same camp grounds the folks did. We got to Missouri, and began the search for Mothers birth place. We felt we got close, but the actual house had long disappeared. We finished the trip East in Springfield, Missouri, where the folks ended their trip.

On our way back to California, as Marv had promised, we stopped again in the town of Follett where it seemed that kin-folks from miles around were there for the reunion. Dinner was following church services on Sunday morning. One of Bill's closest friend, Jim Garrison, was a pastor of a church in Gage, Oklahoma - about 15 miles from Follett. So we went to church there to surprise Jim, and had a nice visit with him before we returned to the reunion. Boy!! do those Texans know how to throw a Texas Potluck Dinner. We were a little late getting back from Gage, but there was still lots of food to eat, and people to meet. We stayed at one of

Marv's aunt's place about three days where he parked
his rig in her driveway, and I parked on a lot next to her
house. From Texas, we headed back to California
where Betty and Marv drove to their place on Rocky Top
while Mom and I returned to Fresno for the winter.

In 1990, we bought a new Chevrolet one-ton pick-up
with a big 454 motor. We decided to take it on a drive,
so we headed for Borrego Springs, (near San Diego)
where Betty and Marv lived at that time. While we were
there, the four of us decided we should take another trip
together. This time it was about a two month trip to
Washington D.C.. We elected Betty to be our tour
director, so she got out all her books and maps, lined out
the trip, and marked all the interesting places we should
go to and visit. She had about three months to get
prepared since we would leave the first of May.

We decided to meet and make our starting point for the
trip at the little town of Daggett (about 7 miles east of
Barstow). As we were approaching the off ramp for
Daggett, we saw Betty and Marv on the ramp going over
the highway. Our trip from Fresno, and their trip from
Borrego Springs were perfectly timed. Was this an
omen of a successful trip?   I think it was.

We had a reservation for the seasons first train ride from
Durango, Colorado to Silverton. It was a beautiful ride
running along the Animas River. Silverton is the end of
the line, and the old steam engine has to be turned
around while all the people were eating, or just viewing
the town. The train got about half-way to Silverton when
I discovered my keys were not in my pocket where I
usually kept them; I panicked and went bananas. We
had parked our rigs in the parking lot for the train ride,

and I was worried someone would find those keys and would see my new pick-up and trailer headed for tim-buk-2 (as the old saying goes). When we got back to the parking lot, I was relieved to see my rig still parked there. When I walked up to the trailer, there under the step laid my keys.

My sister Betty loved the history of the American Indians. So through all of Arizona and New Mexico, we visited every place that had a feather sticking up. She knew the story of every Indian Chief and every battle ground. I was particularly interested in all the cliff dwellings. We visited one of Mary's aunts, and her two cousins that lived in Kansas. It was here where we learned the real feel of great thunder boomers. They would shake you right out of the car. As we moved along, I cannot remember all the fun places we stopped, and maybe it's a good thing because I would never end this trip.

Moving right along, we spent about three days in Nashville - what an interesting place. Western excitement everywhere, and we took in a lot of shows while we were there. We found trailer space in Maryland, just outside of Washington D.C., and spent eleven days touring Washington. We left on Highway 95 going south through all the land filled with Civil War history. I was amazed at the close range shooting that was involved in those days - they could almost touch hands they were so close.   Continuing south, we went to Kissimmee, Florida, where we suffered in the heat and humidity, and went through another thunder boomer that took out all the parks electricity. My poor little Mary was huddled up in the center of the trailer.

While in Kissimmee we spent four days doing the Disney

and Epcot Center tourist attractions. We then headed west to New Orleans, where we spent several days - New Orleans is a great city. We kept going west to San Antonio, Texas where we visited the famous Alamo; I kept thinking of all those Hollywood stars losing their lives over and over in the movie. Farther west we traveled to Big Bend, Texas where you could just walk across the Rio Grande. At this point the temperature was so high our air conditioners did no good at all in keeping us cool as we headed into New Mexico to the White Sands National Monument. From there onward to Tombstone (AZ) and the O.K. Corral, where a few gunslingers met up with Wyatt Earp, Doc Holiday, and Bat Masterson who cleared out the outlaws. While we were there, a colony of black ants took over the trailer, and no matter what we did we couldn't get rid of them. They survived the winter in Fresno, but when we left for Oregon in the spring, they moved out.

That just about covers our two months on the road with lots of fun and lots of gasoline.

About the first of May, we were on our way back to our little place in Oregon. The lady we bought the trailer from had the yard looking very nice. She had grass planted all around the house, and for several years I hired someone to mow and trim the grass, and pick up the trash and papers. After they moved away, or forget to come and mow, we decided on a new plan. I learned that the park management wanted to know about any changes that were made, and I learned that the best way was to go ahead and do what you wanted and let the chips fall where they may.

First, I started with the grass. I got my sprayer out and

was spraying Round Up on the lawn to get rid of it.
When the manager passed by, he motioned a thumbs-
up because he thought I was spraying fertilizer on it.
After about a week-and-a-half, I took my weed eater and
took the grass right down to the ground, and then spread
bark all over it. The manager passed by again and said
the owner was unhappy about taking the grass out. I
told him if she wanted to take care of it (by paying for
new grass), I would put it back. Case closed.

Next I got a decorative cement form, and built a nice
path around the west side of the house. I put four
cement blocks next to the edge of the road, and then
added a big flower pot filled with flowers. Then we
added several other flower pots around the yard, and
filled them too. I added sprinklers around the yard so
that all the pots had water. In the fall, we pulled out the
summer flowers and added something that would stay
green through the winter months. We then shut-off the
water, drained the lines, and headed south to Fresno for
the winter.

The first of May the following year, we would repeat the
process. We had a favorite flower nursery about
fourteen miles away in Woodburn, Oregon, so we would
go up there and fill the car with nice healthy plants. We
then replanted all the pots, turned on the water, and we
were ready for another trailer trip. Or so we thought - I
found that the moles had discovered that under the
cement stones in the new sidewalk was a good place to
find bugs; so there was some repair work to be done.

Mary and I discovered that our 26 foot trailer was
showing some serious signs of wear. We had found
some dry rot in the front that would be expensive to

repair, and the tires had a lot of years and miles on them and needed to be replaced as well. So we decided to look around and see what was available. With our old trailer as a trade-in, we found a 24 foot Terry fifth-wheel that would look nice with our new pick-up. It was the right amount of cash so we bought it.

New Wheels –
The Open Road Was Ahead One More Time!

A house becomes a home when you can write "I love you" on the furniture.

Dust if you must
"Dust if you must, but wouldn't it be better,
to paint a picture or write a letter,
bake a cake or plant a seed,
ponder the difference between want and need?

Dust if you must, but there's not much time,
with rivers to swim and mountains to climb,

James William Huckaby
"Mr. Huck"

music to hear and books to read, friends to
cherish and life to lead.

Dust if you must, but the world's out there
With the sun in your eyes, the wind in your hair,
A flutter of snow, a shower of rain.
This day will not come around again.

Dust if you must, but bear in mind,
old age will come and it's not kind.
And when you go - and go you must -
You, yourself, will make more dust!"

- Rose Milligan

"All flesh shall perish together
And man shall turn again into dust"
Job 34:15

"It's not what you gather, but what you scatter
that tells what kind of life you have lived."

- Helen Walton

Chapter Twenty-Two

CONFESSIONS AND DO-OVERS

*"Feelings can be like wild animals, we underrate how
fierce they are until we've opened their cages."*
- Richard Paul Evans

You may have noticed that all of the quotes at the
beginning of each chapter are from Best Selling Author
Richard Paul Evans of Salt lake City, Utah. I discovered
Mr. Evans work years ago when I picked up a little book
called The Christmas Box Miracle. I was so impressed
with his quotations that I picked up another of his books
The Carousel, then The Gift, The Sunflower, The Letter,
Finding Noel, The Last Promise, The Timepiece, and A
Perfect Day. Now you should know I read like I type,
very slowly, so it took me several weeks to read all these
books. I enjoyed the stories in the books, but what
totally impressed me were all the quotations in each of
the nine books. It seemed that each one reminded me
of a certain memory I had in my life. I had to find some
way to share them with my family and friends.

I went over to our family drug store and bought a paper
tablet, then went to the library and checked out all nine
books, brought them home, and copied every quote onto
that tablet. I thought someday maybe I could do
something with them, so I tossed the pad on my desk
along with a lot of other stuff. Periodically I would pick it
up and read through it, and then toss it back on the desk.
I would take it with us when we went back and forth to
Oregon, and almost wore it out just carrying it around.

When we moved here to Lodi it was one of the first things I located and tossed on my new desk. At last I have done what I have intended to do all these years, and that is to share these quotes with you. I hope that you can see how each one was important to me. The paper tablet is in very sad shape now; the front cover was lost long ago, and it was torn in half so the back half could be used for other things. The pages that are left have had the quotes scratched off as they were also used for other things; in fact there are very few quotes left. I sometimes think I should call my book The Tablet from all of the quotes I wrote in that note pad.

My concern now is, "How much trouble am I in for using all of Mr. Evens quotes in my book?" This book is not for sale, and is totally for the enjoyment of my friends and relatives. Maybe you, Mr. Evans, are a little bit responsible for this story because your books were so darn great. Let me leave you with a quotation from one of your own books:

"It's one thing to order an execution,
it's a whole different matter to swing the axe."
- Richard Paul Evans

Confessions

Confession number one:

War!! I quickly learned two things about war.

First is that young men go to war, and second that young men die in war. In my war they died by the hundreds of thousands. Most of those who survived would probably describe war as the nearest thing to hell that they ever experienced. I was on a U.S. Ship for a 3 year cruse furnished by my Uncle Sam searching for Japanese submarines. Once when we were searching for Jap subs during the invasion of Tarawa I heard from the bridge there's a body out on the water. Shortly, there was another, then another, and another. These were the bodies of Marines that were aboard the troop ship I could see in the distance.

I learned much later that these brave men climbed down the nets into the landing crafts and headed for the beach. When they were about 150 yards from the beach, the craft hit a coral reef that it couldn't get over. So they lowered the ramp where they were stopped, the Marines were forced out in water up to their arm pits holding their guns over their heads - they were easy targets and the Japanese picked them off one by one. Landing crafts up and down the reef did the same thing with the same result, and then they headed back to the troop ship for their next load of Marines.

The bay was bloody with hundreds of floating bodies. These were the bodies our ship bumped out of the way as we were searching for submarines. I wondered if any of those bodies were the friends that signed up for the Marines the same day I signed up for the Navy. Because of this story, along with the large number of personal friends that never returned home from that war, for the next 60 years I have lived with a certain amount of guilt about surviving it. I weep for them when I go to a Veterans celebration - I stand not for myself, but I stand for them. They are after all the real heroes of the war.

Today over a thousand World War II veterans will die;

the next time you see an old man hobbling down the sidewalk with his cane or walker, take a few minutes to ask him if he was one of the lucky few to survive my war. If he says yes, give him a big "high five", tell him thanks and good job, swat him on his butt, and send him on his way.

> *"Sometimes to move forward*
> *we must be willing to look back."*
> *- Richard Paul Evans*

Confession number 2:

According to my dictionary, as I stated before, a memoir is a narrative composed from personal experience; an autobiography. Basically I have tried to hold to the truth; occasionally a little lie here and there just to hold your interest, but generally all of it is true and about me. However I must also tell you I have tried to include a little love story along the way. If you caught it I am very happy because that is what it was for. If you didn't, let me point out a few helper points.

First I know that I fell in love with my Mary at the college Mid Winter ball. She looked so beautiful. When she said yes to my proposal, and then yes at the alter; I loved her even more. During the war she was so patient with our years of separation, and an inspiration to me on the ship; someone I anxiously wanted to come home to. She never complained about our one room apartment, and was an angel taking care of our little angel Connie. She was always there with the other children when they needed her. She was by my side when we bought anything: a house, a car, or even a pair of socks. We were there for each other when we lost both our parents, and she taught me and all of our kids how to love with the Agape love of Jesus Christ - that kind of love is what holds my entire family together. Because of that love, Mary and I have danced together for 70 years now, and the music still plays loud and strong.

"You don't stop dancing cause you get old,
you get old cause you stop dancing."

"When one tries to hide love,
one gives the best evidence of it's existence."

- Richard Paul Evans

DO-OVERS

Do you know what a do-over is? It is something like, "I wonder what would have happened if I turned right instead of left." One of the areas of my life that I have wondered about was our decision not to go back to school as soon as I got out of the Navy, but to go to work instead. My goal would have been to become a Civil Engineer: that would take a full 4 years of school if I didn't have to work, and a great deal longer if I did. Mary would have to get a job to help out with the finances, and we would have had to postpone our family plans - the birth of our Connie. We would probably have ended up living in the same one room apartment for several more years, and who knows how long before we could have our little Connie.

No, No, No.

Mary wanted to become a Mommy, and she didn't want

to fool around about it. In fact, Mary wanted us to try for
a baby during the three months the ship was in Seattle
for the two year overhaul. Which we did, but the eggs
went south when they should have gone north, or
something. A month later Mary wrote with tears in her
eyes (I think I saw tear drops on the letter), that we
would have to wait to try again at another time.

So what would we have gained if I did go back to
school?

I would have ended up in some engineer's office making
a few bucks more maybe. We possibly could have eaten
Rib Eye instead of round steak (and break the old family
tradition that stopped with me), and maybe a new car
instead of a used one; but would it have been fair to my
two old family station wagons that we all loved.

I think not, I think what we did was right, and I would
never change it. I think of the fun and pleasure I had
running my first survey crew - the memory is still there
65 years later. Besides I think we did exactly what God
intended us to do.

I have another do-over that I think about occasionally,
and wonder what it would be like if we had made a
different decision. It has to do with that night Mary and I
sat in the car in the forks in the road: one fork going to
Fresno, the other going back to Belridge. As you may
remember, we chose to go to Fresno.

What could we have expected if we had chosen
Belridge?

First off, I never heard of anyone working in the oil fields being wealthy - oil people of wealth lived in Los Angeles and worked in the big buildings in the city. Only once in a while did you ever see them in the field. Most field workers made a comfortable living. Most on retirement ended up with a house in Bakersfield that was paid for, and pittance of a retirement for the rest of their life. Not the greatest way to live your life, but it was how my parents lived their life

.

There is one thing I have lived with all these years in regards to our decision to go to Fresno that I will share with you. I believe that if we had been at Belridge, Old Doc Dykes, our family doctor for years, could have delivered our little Connie to us as a healthy baby. I always felt that the doctor we had made a misjudgment some where.

Would I do that do-over if I could? IN A MINUTE.

If I Had My Life to Live Over

*"I'd dare to make more mistakes next time.
I'd relax. I would limber up.
I would be sillier than I have been this trip.
I would take fewer things seriously.
I would take more chances.
I would take more trips.
I would climb more mountains and swim more rivers.
I would eat more ice cream and less beans.
I would perhaps have more actual troubles but I'd
have fewer imaginary ones.
You see, I'm one of those people who live sensibly
and sanely hour after hour, day after day.
Oh, I've had my moments and if I had it to do over*

again, I'd have more of them.
In fact, I'd try to have nothing else.
Just moments. One after another,
instead of living so many years ahead of each day.
I've been one of those people who never go anywhere
without a thermometer, a hot water bottle, a raincoat
and a parachute.
If I had my life to live over, I would start barefoot
earlier in the spring and stay that way later in the fall.
If I had it to do again, I would travel lighter next time.
I would go to more dances.
I would ride more merry-go-rounds.
I would pick more daisies."
- Nadine Stair

And babe, we'll do it together one more time.

"And now, to him who is able to do exceedingly,
abundantly above all that we ask or think,
to him be the glory in Christ Jesus
for now and evermore. Amen."
Ephesians 3:20-21

Last night was Halloween and the goblins' were out in force, each with their bag of goodies so loaded it was dragging on the ground dropping little mints along the sidewalk. Tommy and his girlfriend Jessica, from Bend Oregon, spent the night with Bill and Cathy, and we were there visiting with them. They were here in California to pick up a Siberian Husky puppy that Tommy had gotten for Jessica. It had been at least a year since the last time we saw Tommy, and we enjoyed the visit very much.

The first of November followed Halloween this year, like

that was a big surprise. What is a surprise is where did the year go? Each day and each year brings me nearer to that great finale, that's in the future. The time of death is not determined by anyone or anything here on earth; that decision is made by the Councils of Heaven. When we have done all that God has in mind for us to do, then and only then will he take us home; and not one second before. As Paul put it:

"David, after he had served his own generation by the will of God, fell asleep" Acts 13:36

I often wondered how I would grow old. I kind of just jumped in, and there I was, on old man plain and simple. I always claimed that God never made any mistakes, but there are two things he could have done to make life a little easier.

First he could have given us a little hand book entitled, "How to Raise Children," and then one, "How Men Should Grow Old." Now with the children thing I used a little bit of my own theology. I went to my Bible in the Genesis and read where God put Adam and Eve in the Garden of Eden to tend to it. He told them not to eat from the tree of the Knowledge of Good and Evil. Then one day when Adam walks by, and Eve says, "Come in for a piece of hot apple pie."

ZING BANG BOOM, you know the rest of the story.

If God had trouble with his children, I could expect that mine might not be perfect. I don't remember a specific time when I decided it was time to start growing old. It probably caught me when I was walking down the 18th fairway dragging a hand cart full of clubs headed for the green, and then I realized next time I was going to ride in a cart. Sometimes it seemed more pressing if my game had been more in the water or in a lot of high ruff. I think when naps came more frequently, especially when I was watching television, and my cane walking stick became more useful as a cane, in fact I use it all the time now. I don't know what happened, but all of a sudden there it is - old age.

I hope that I have not embarrassed anyone by the way it happened, if I did I am so sorry. Somewhere in this book I have mentioned the saying that children should be seen and not heard - this is also true for old men. I find that it is best not to talk to much; it's the easiest way to stay out of trouble. I have never been known to say two words if one will do the job anyway. Sometimes when I'm with a group, I have been known to set in a chair pretending to be asleep, and not have to say anything all evening.

And now I have said November is here, and that winter is closing in; and that my winter is also closing in - I think it is time to bring this book to a close. I hope that you have enjoyed reading it as much as I have enjoyed writing it. Remember it was all written in love, and since it has been written in love you are going to see some mistakes along the way. You'll see spelling and punctuation mistakes, as well as some of the dates and years may be off. With my bad memory and my age, I am entitled to be wrong; it goes with the territory.

And I also claim the right to tell a small lie occasionally if it makes the story better. So now that you have just about finished the book: overlook the errors, and don't be too critical of its author.

James William Huckaby
"Mr. Huck"

"If you have to tell someone you're famous, you're not."

"The only promise of childhood is that it will end."

- Richard Paul Evans

I wonder what kind of a parent I've been. I did my best. Sometimes I suppose I even got it right. Kids don't come with owners manuals. You have to figure each of them out, and by the time you do, their gone. I pray that I didn't do them too much harm, and hope for their sakes, that they will forgive me someday if I did.

My family: I need to say a word to them.

They have allowed me to be the Patriarch of this family for many years, and each of them has been the pride of my heart. Will and Mary, Tim and Carol, Randy and Sue, and Bill and Cathy have each had an influence on the direction of my life one way or the other. They all have to be admired for the different lives they have lived. They have all been successful at the professions they have chosen. They all have beautiful homes and fine families. The total of their children is an even dozen; that in itself is something to be proud of. I'm sure that they have had their problems, but they have stuck together and worked them out. I am proud of them for the way they have all kept their marriage vows, the way they have kept the faith through the years, and I am sure God is well pleased. I hope that you enjoy the book because you are an important part of it

After 70 years of dancing with the same girl, I am tongue tied on what to say. The little ladybug that I asked to go to the Mid Winter Ball became a KEEPER. The keeper was that cute little red haired ladybug – my "Pinkie", with a white blouse, a red plaid mini-skirt, white bobby socks, and brown and white saddle shoes that got on my bus so many years ago.

Mary, you have been very precious to me, our love for each other grows a little bit more each year. So I'm just going to say to my Mary, "Let's plan to meet in that great Ball Room in the sky for our last dance to the Hallelujah Chorus. I'll love you then as I love you today – with all my heart. Thank you for everything you made so precious; I also thank you for the way you have kept me humble and loyal to my first and greatest love: The Lord Jesus Christ."

> *"Some of us live and some of us die*
> *and some day God's going to tell us why.*
> *So open your hearts, and grow with what life sends,*
> *we'll meet again at the festival of friends.*
> *I'll see you there."*
> *- Author unknown*

I pray that in some way, one of you may have been blessed because of the way I have lived my life.

Mr. Huck.

"A LITTLE TO THE RIGHT"
To the cross and the Lords right hand.
Don't let your power lines miss these blessings.

James William Huckaby
"Mr. Huck"

"The Lord is my strength and my song;
he has become my salvation
Shouts of joy and victory resounds
in the tents of the righteous:
The Lord's right hand is lifted high;
the Lord's right hand has done mighty things."

PSALMS 118:14-16

EPILOGUE

Rescued from the archives of my laptop computer.

Here we go again, one more time. It has been over two years that I stopped working on my story. We were getting unhappy at the Vintage: the rent was going up, the food was tasting the same at every meal, and I was having a very big "I don't like you" with the managers. So we gave a two weeks notice and pulled the plug.

We are out in the street without a boat so what to do next.

We looked at all kinds of rentals, and were not happy with anything we saw. Bill said, "Dad I moved you from Fresno to the Vintage, and I will move you out of the Vintage to a rental; but, when you get mad at the owner for raising the rent, you are going to move yourself. Why don't you buy a house and I will never have to move you again?"

We looked at a lot of houses, and each one of them seemed to have things that needed fixing, but might be alright. Bill said, "Just keep looking till you make sure it's what you really want." Finally, we stopped at 2230 Giannoni Way. Mary walked in, looked all through the house, and then yelled, "Where do I sign?"

She was sure it was exactly what she wanted. I had a long long talk with God about an 88 year old man getting a 30 year mortgage to buy a house. He sort of said, "Quit worrying; GO FOR IT!"; which we did. In the deal, Mary got to buy a house full of new furniture (the house was a model home when the housing tract first opened), which was good because we got rid of everything when we moved into the Vintage.

Now getting back to this Memoirs thing: it was a total mess when I last left it. I had rewritten a good portion of it, and I had changed the order of thirteen of the twenty-two chapters. I had also lost chapter fifteen when I stopped. Three weeks ago, Bill called and said that he found a good deal on a computer and a new printer if I wanted it. I told him to get it, and while he was setting it up on my desk, I asked him if we could do something with my story? It took Bill all afternoon rambling through the archives to get my book, once again, organized so I could continue working like mad where I had left off. After about three more weeks, I finally think I have something that I can print. I tried to get rid of all the misspelled words, a ton of commas, and a few ????. But I find that I have over two more years that I don't know what to do with; could there be another Memoirs Part Two???.

I don't think so! However, there are a couple things I would like to add to my life span trip.

In September of 2012, the kids threw me a surprise ninety-year old birthday party - it was great to see all my friends there. I haven't as yet figured out which was the greatest surprise: the party, or the fact that I lived to see ninety years. Both of my parents lived to be eighty two years old. I always figured I would possibly live about the same, and was happy with that thought. In as much as I have never yet figured God out, this September I will be ninety-two. Mary and I will be married seventy years, and boy what a memorable trip that has been. And the